Adoption

The Best Gift

A handbook for prospective adoptive parents

by

Nikki Biers

A Division of Wise Bear, Inc.
Los Angeles, California

7/5/13

Dear Dr. Dwyer,

With Thanks for all you have
done to help Charlie.

You have our sincere gratitude!

Warmest regards,

Nikki Biro

Adoption, The Best Gift

Printed in the United States of America.

Published by Wise Bear Media, a division of Wise Bear, Inc., Los Angeles, California www.wisebearmedia.com

ISBN: 978-0-9830688-3-9

eBook (mobi) ISBN: 978-0-9830688-4-6

eBook (epub) ISBN: 978-0-9830688-5-3

LCCN: 2011936847

Praise for Nikki and Michael Biers and Best Gift Adoptions

In the pages of this book you will discover a woman who lives by example; who walks the walk as well as talks the talk. My husband and I had 4 children and our thoughts about adoption drifted in and out like the tide. Everything happens for a reason and people come into our lives to teach us, I have discovered. It was quite by accident that I met Nikki, I thought. Now I know that is not the case. She and her husband Michael changed the course of our family's life by presenting us with an opportunity that will be forever indelible in our very existence. It is because of them and the ease with which they brought unto us our fifth child, Olivia Luna, that a match, and adoption and a blessing for all of us took place. A "situation" like this, a process that can be harrowing at best, was made effortless by a woman who only wants the very best and understands the most basic human need for a child, a family. She found one for this tiny human being and our already established tribe. And, we have found one in her.

Joely Fisher, Actress

The experience of working with you on the adoption of my baby has been one of the most wonderful of my life. I'm .so grateful to you, not first for my beautiful new daughter, but for showing me that its possible to combine real professionalism with compassion in such a graceful and wonderfully effective way.

I interviewed several offices that handle adoptions in Los Angeles, including the most famous lawyers I could find and their staffs… and to this day I'm not sure I would have even continued pursuing adoption if I hadn't met you. You are the only reason I decided to work with your office, and - in spite of years of knowing I wanted a family - you're the single most compelling force that helped me get from loving the concept of it to letting the reality of it take.

You have a very inspiring way of helping people really discover what they want and need while allowing for every imaginable fear and anxiety. I guess what impressed me most is that you were able to maintain the exact sane enthusiasm for nurturing while keeping the paperwork proceeding, the momentum going, and the phone calls answered for so many clients with so many different problems all at once. On top of it all, you never once lost your sense of humor which I found really astounding, since I lose mine many times a day and it's supposed to be my field of expertise.

I've met a lot of business people in my career, but not many who's mode of doing business is one I really aspire to. I hope my new daughter will have a chance to get to know you better and that you can teach us some of your secrets.

Cathy Guisewite,
Creator of the "Cathy" Comic Strip

Best Gift Adoption is the best thing that ever happened to us! When we decided to adopt, we met with lawyers and agencies - and found both to be too impersonal for our tastes. Then we found Best Gift Adoptions. Actually, we found Nikki and Michael. They guided us with love and the understanding of the emotions that come with the process. They always assured us that, "the right child will come to you." *They worked tirelessly for us. They were always available, always positive, always working to match us with the perfect birth mother. And, just as importantly to us, they nurtured the birthmother through her experience. With strong and gentle hands they coached us from our first meeting with our birth mother, to the moment we cut the cord in the delivery room. In the end, they brought us our most precious joy - a beautiful baby girl. And four years later, we consider Nikki and Michael part of our family, too. They are true angels for both birth mothers and adoptive parents.*

Kimm and Greg D.

I highly recommend 'Best Gift Adoptions.' I met Nikki 10 years ago when I decided to place a child, in the end I choose to parent that baby. 5 years later I needed to call her again to place my second child. I had a few horror stories with other agencies and families, but Nikki comforted me and found me the most perfect, dream family. They were every single thing that I wanted and more, in a family for my child, it was amazing, since I was quite picky. I still keep in touch with Nikki and value her highly as a dear friend. I can assure you that no agency, lawyer, or facilitator will show you the love, support, encouragement, and respect that Nikki Biers will. This woman is fabulous. She does everything to help you, and then some. She does not view adoption as a careless business agreement, but values and loves all parties involved deeply. Nikki will refer you to every service available to you and be there at any moment for anything you need. This woman truly is a miracle worker. Many agencies, and facilitators can be wonderful people, but none seem to show the level of compassion, loyalty, sincerity and dedication as Nikki Biers does. Words can never express my gratitude for this woman and her company. If you are in a situation that you are faced with an unplanned pregnancy, it can be very scary. Nikki calms all your fears, she will not force you to choose a family from a small group of adoptive parents, she will search until she finds the PERFECT fit for you. She is a wonderful humanitarian and a great friend, I love this woman as if she were my very own mother. So again, Best Gift Adoption, is highly personal, deeply dedicated, and well above the rest in terms of the care and attention that you will receive. I recommend them with all my heart and soul.

Amanda S.

I have used this adoption office. I had a baby young and found Nikki and Michael Biers. They are the sweetest people you will ever meet. I still keep in touch with them and that has been for 12 years. If something is wrong they will do what they can to help solve the problem. Sometimes families do not follow the agreement they promised to follow, but that is rare to happen. It just happened to me, but she did what she could to make it better. She will come out to meet the person who wants to give their baby up for adoption and be there for you through the whole process. I highly recommend Best Gift Adoption if adoption is what you are interested in.

Jennifer P.

Thank you so much for allowing me to have the honor of being one of the first to read your book. It was truly a gift that came into my life at the perfect time. It answered questions I didn't even know I needed to ask. Anyone thinking or in the process of adoption should read this book. It's an amazing adoption guide to help couples get through the process at every step, from finding an adoption facilitator to being at the hospital for the birth of your baby. I enjoyed the personal stories you shared as well as the feelings. Allows adopting parents to feel like their emotions are normal.

Nicole H.

This book will answer all your questions regarding the adoption process. Nikki and Michael worked with us every step of the way through our own adoption. I wish this book would have been available as we went through our adoption. Reading it brought me back to that time when we had all those questions about we had along the way. Also, this book faces adoption from a realistic point of view. There are real people involved who are forging a new family. This book will help both adoptive parents and birth parents understand what to expect from each other as they go through the process. This book is a blessing and the next best thing to working with Nikki and Michael directly.

Karen R.

Acknowledgements

I'd like to thank my children for the lessons they've taught me and the joys they've brought me. Great thanks to Dr. Carolyn Conger, who nudged me to take the writing class that kept me on point to finish this book. Thank you to Kim Calder and Chiwan Choi whose guidance in class was invaluable and, to the members of my class whose input and support kept me on track.

To the attorneys and agencies and social workers who have been dedicated to supporting our adoptive families and birthmothers and provided legal services for them.

And, finally, thank you more than I can express, to the adoptive families and birthparents who have allowed us the privilege of participating with them during this very personal experience. We are deeply grateful for being allowed to share the births and adoption processes of their precious babies.

Dedication

This book is dedicated to my husband, Michael for his endless support and belief in me, and in this project. To our children, Jimmy, Emma, Charlie and Nika, who are the reasons for it, and our greatest blessings. And, to their birthmothers who allowed us to parent their precious babies and entrusted them to our care.

Table of Contents

Drug And/Or Alcohol Use During Pregnancy

Other Health Issues With The Baby

Who Is She?

What Is She Looking For In A Family For Her Baby?

How Does The Match Happen?

How Long Before The Baby Is Born Do We Match?

Will Someone Be With Us When We Meet Her?

What Do We Talk About?

What Happens Between The Match And The Birth Of The Baby?

What Happens When The Baby Has Been Born Before The Match?

When Should We Start Buying Things? What About A Shower?

When Do We Tell Our Other Children And Family Members We're Going To Adopt?

What Are The Birthmother's Rights?

Who Will Be With Her When She Delivers The Baby?

If I/We Are Allowed In The Delivery Room, Who Will Hold The Baby First After He/She is Born?

How Much Time Will We Spend With The Baby? How Much Time Will We Spend With The Birthmother?

Should We Give Her A Gift?

What Do We Do If She Wants Time Alone With The Baby?

How Long Will She Be There?

When Can We Take The Baby Home?

What Has To Happen For The Legal Process At The Hospital?

What Happens If Something Is Wrong With The Baby?

Post Birth Contact With Birthparents

What Do We Do If the Birthmother Calls?

Remember What Your Birthmother Is Giving You

Should The Baby Know He/She Is Adopted?

When And How Do We Tell Him/Her?

What Do We Tell Him About His/Her Birthmother?

Forward

Wonderful news that Nikki Biers has written this much needed book on adoption. Knowing Nikki for over 30 years and working closely with her, I know how dedicated she is to helping potential adoptive parents and birthmothers find each other. Because this is a delicate subject, at so many levels, Nikki has done a masterful job of addressing every issue in an easy to understand and thorough way. This book will help every person considering adoption take the proper steps to a successful and stress-free adoption experience.

Ignorance is not bliss, but the cause of unlimited problems. Proper knowledge offered from a person with vast experience on the subject, prevents problems and offers the guidance necessary to assist each family wishing to adopt, helping them to form and complete an adoption plan.

Love is what we all seek and having loving parents is the greatest blessing that any person can have. Our earliest years are the forming years and with so many infants and children in need of caring and devoted families, adoption is often the way to provide the gift of family for little ones and waiting parents.

Every question is answered in Nikki's comprehensive guidebook, which I whole-heartedly recommend. My prayer is that all children and all who desire to parent find each other and create a positive family experience together, forever.

Dr. Terry Cole-Whittaker

Introduction

"The Best Gift" is a song I heard years ago on a Barbra Streisand Christmas album. It is a sweet song about the birth of a baby. I have loved it since the first time I heard it. Of course, it's appropriate for every newborn, but I felt a strong attraction to the lyrics when we adopted our first baby.

The best gift that I ever got
didn't really weigh a lot.
It didn't have a ribbon 'round
and it sometimes made a terrible sound.

The best of all, it seems to me
wasn't 'neath the Christmas tree,
and yet, I guess I'd have to say
that it made all the other presents twice as gay.

The best gift that I've ever known
I'd always wanted most to own.

Yet, in my dreams of sugar and spice
I never thought it could be so nice.

The best gift that I'll ever get
was sometimes dry and sometimes wet.
was usually pink, though often-times red
As it lay so innocently in its' bed.

The best gift of the year to me
the one I hold most dear to me,
The gift that simply drove me wild
was a tiny, newborn child.

Music and Lyrics by Lan O'Kun

When we opened our current adoption facilitation office, The Best Gift Adoptions, Inc. seemed the natural name for the company.

I have been working in adoption since 1991. Since the birth of our first baby, I have known this is my work. I am blessed to have my children; four biological children who are now adults and 3 adopted. Many prospective adoptive parents have struggled with infertility for several years, and have told me they don't know if they can love a child who is not biologically related to them. It is a joy to see them when they hold their babies for the first time, and all the fear and doubt disappears. There is a kind of "knowing" of this tiny person, sometimes at the moment of meeting the birthmother and/or at birth. The result is immediate and overwhelming love for our children. I can tell this to families over and over again... and I do...but until they meet their little ones, it is only talk.

It's a great privilege to write about adoption. It's the topic about which I have the most passion. This book chronicles the practical steps to adopting, along with some of our adoptive families and birthmother's experiences. I hope it proves helpful to all involved in or investigating this wonderful adventure.

1.

Why Adopt?

There are as many reasons to adopt as there are potential adoptive families. Each family's story is unique.

Infertility

The most common reason most families come to adoption is infertility. For families who have experienced the difficulties, emotions, stress and frustration of infertility treatment with no success, the need to mend and heal is the first and most important order of business. At the point when a family has begun to resolve this, they may begin to consider adoption as the way to build or complete their families.

A few years ago, one of our clients referred friends who had been in fertility treatment for some time. They met with us on a Saturday afternoon. They both cried as they told us they had just, earlier that week, found out that there was no chance they could become pregnant. Although they were devastated, they had anticipated this result. They had been considering adoption during the last part of their treatment. When they received the news, they decided to begin investigating.

Tom and Lucy told us they were so ready to be parents and that this was the thing they wanted most and had prayed for, for a very long time. They felt they had been grieving their infertility for some time; and although the process had left them pretty raw, they were ready to move forward. They said they were open to any race or gender baby and they wanted to begin the process immediately.

Two days later, on Monday, we received a call from a local hospital. There had been a baby girl born to a woman from a South Sea island that morning. Jean was married and had 4 other children. She and her husband had discussed adoption for their expected baby. They had a limited income and felt they could not adequately provide for the children they had, and had decided to place the baby for adoption at birth.

Jean was a flight attendant with a major airline and was in Los Angeles for a 2-day layover. She had not been receiving prenatal care and thought she was about 6 months pregnant. She and a co-worker took a trip to a local mall during their layover and while they were shopping, her water broke. When she arrived at the hospital she discovered that the baby was actually full-term and was born weighing in at over 9 lbs.

I went to the hospital and met with her. Jean told me what she would like in a family for her baby. I showed her some letters from potential families. Since I didn't yet have a letter from Tom and Lucy, I told her a little about them. I knew from our conversation the previous week, that Tom and Lucy had some connection to Jean's home country. After considering the families, Jean chose Tom and Lucy.

When they arrived at the hospital, there was an immediate connection with Jean. Tom, Lucy, and birthmother Jean, spent several hours learning about each other and discovered many common beliefs and interests. When Tom left to gather things for the baby, Lucy and Jean shared care of baby Lilly. They had lots of time to learn about each other. Tom and Lucy still have periodic contact through letters and photos with Jean and her family.

Later, Lucy told me that on that morning, she had been out for a walk and had been praying that she was ready now for a child to join her family. Since then, they have gone on to complete their family with the adoption of their second daughter.

Second Marriages

Some families may be in a second marriage, where one partner has school-age or teen children, and the other has not experienced being a parent. This was the case with my family. My first husband and I divorced when the oldest of our 4 children was 16 and the youngest was 5. I was single for 9 years and remarried at 44. My husband, Michael, had never been married and, although he was a wonderful step-father to my children, wanted to start a family with me.

After 1 ½ years attempting to become pregnant, we both felt adoption was a great option for us, especially since I wasn't getting any younger. I had always wanted to adopt a child, and Michael felt the same, so we began the process, and adopted our first son a year later. We now have 3 beautiful children, along with our 4 adult kids, 4 grandchildren and 2 great-grandbabies. Adopting our first son was the inspiration for my beginning my work in adoption.

Single Parent Adoption

Many singles, at a certain point, want very much to parent and are drawn to adoption as one of the options open to them. It is a huge undertaking when you are looking at the idea of raising a child without a partner. Many of our single adoptive parents wait until they are comfortable taking on this responsibility. Although it is much more common for women who are single to adopt than for men, we had a case 2 years ago, with a loving, kind man who came to us after a divorce. He wanted a child very much and was a professional man in his 30's who didn't know what the prospects were for another marriage. Both Michael and I fell in love with who he was, and, although we told him it was very uncommon for a birthmother to want to place her baby with a single male, we would try if he wanted to continue. Paul waited a long time . . . about 2 years with no interest from a birthmother.

He was discouraged, but stayed with us. We then received a call from one of the attorneys with whom we work. He said there was a baby who had been born in another state, and placed with a single mom. She flew home with the baby, and on the night she arrived, the baby turned blue. She took him to the hospital and when she learned he had a heart problem, she called the attorney and asked him to find another family. She felt she couldn't devote the time necessary to accommodate the baby's needs.

The attorney called me and we talked about Paul. I had mentioned Paul earlier and had sent him a profile of his. We discussed whether this birthmother would be willing to consider a single dad. Paul's work allowed him a flexible schedule that would permit him time to meet the baby's needs; and, he had family nearby who were anxious to help. The attorney consulted with the birthmother about him. She asked to speak with Paul and after she did, she called back and said she felt very comfortable with him and wanted to go forward.

The baby has had several surgeries since, and Paul and his family have provided a constant stream of love and support. Paul's mom moved in with him and the baby. As much as Paul is blessed to have the opportunity to parent this baby, this little guy is a lucky boy to have such constant love and devotion; and as a result, he is thriving, walking and talking, and Paul can't stop bragging about him. It has been a joy and a privilege to see this family grow together and to see Paul's unwavering commitment to his son.

We have also had many successful adoptions with single moms. Some birthmothers are happy to consider placing their babies with single women. Some may be single moms and be raising their other children on their own. They may feel that since they are doing it, other single women can do it too. Some birthmothers may not have had successful relationships with men and may prefer working with a single mother.

Can Same Sex Couples Adopt?

Same sex couples often have fears of judgment and criticism when they think about adopting. Their journey can be a little more difficult because some birthmothers are less likely to place their babies with them, than with other, more traditional families.

However, we have had very good success with our same-sex families, both male and female.

One of our male couples had been waiting for several months when we got a call from college student, Sally. She asked, specifically for a same sex couple. She had many friends who were in same sex relationships and she knew that it was harder for them to find a baby to adopt. Sally's boyfriend, Joe was on board with the plan. Sally and Joe met with us and, after studying profiles, they chose our clients, Sam and Mark. They loved that Sam and Mark had many of the same interests and belief systems. The next day they spoke by phone, and their conversation was warm and easy. Sam and Mark came into town, from out of state, to meet Sally and Joe. They stayed in touch regularly by phone throughout the remainder of the pregnancy. Sam and Mark were with Sally and Joe for the birth of their baby. After returning home with their little girl, they are still in contact with Sally, through letters and photos.

Although it may take longer to find the right birthmother, please investigate with a professional and don't give up on the idea because you are fearful it won't happen. Babies need families and there are many birthmothers who are very comfortable placing with a same-sex family. Although every family dynamic is different, the one thing that is true and unchanging is "family", and there are many little ones in need of families to love them. Some potential families are skeptical when I tell them that. My response is, "Wait and see!"

Common Fears About Adopting

The idea of adoption comes, often with great joy, and with a fair amount of skepticism and fear.

What If I Can't Love An Adopted Child?

I have not met too many adoptive families who have not experienced this worry. Although it's hard to imagine loving an adopted child in the same way you would love a biological child, this is a good time to talk with families who have adopted children. Until you hold your baby in your arms, the concept may be difficult to absorb. It's painful to allow yourself to invest in believing this can be a reality, especially if you've experienced failed infertility treatments. We, and most adoption offices, will be happy to refer you to adoptive families who have experienced the same worry. It can be helpful to talk with someone who has been where you are, and have gone on to successfully adopt a child. As stated before, I was blessed with four biological children during my first marriage. When Michael and I decided to learn more about adoption, I was concerned about whether I could feel the same kind of love for an adopted child. I didn't want my adopted child/children to feel that my feelings for them were different or somehow less. This fear kept me up some nights. For my husband, it was a bit different. This was his first child. He expressed the fear that he might not feel the same joy and love for this child as he would for a biological child. We talked about this many times before we found the birthmother of our son, Jimmy.

I have a beautiful photo of the first time Michael saw his son when Jimmy was born. He was waiting in the lobby outside the delivery room. A friend was able to capture his face when he looked in the isolette with tears in his eyes as I wheeled Jimmy out of the Delivery Room.

I was also somewhat surprised to realize that my feelings for Jimmy were exactly the same as for my older children. He was ours. That was it! Any fears to the contrary were dissolved and our love for him only grew more intense as he grew and developed his own unique personality.

Be gentle with yourselves. Allow the fear, but keep moving forward. Talk to as many adoptive families as you can during this time, because when you have your baby, you will be the one telling the next potential family your experience and sharing the joy of your new addition.

What If It Never Happens For Me?

Michael and I and almost every adoptive family we know have reported that same fear. After years of infertility treatment and/or trying to conceive a baby, the reality of parenthood seems unlikely or impossible. The thing about adoption is that there is almost certainly a baby at the end of that tunnel. The longer you have been trying, the harder that is to visualize, but it is essential to picture yourself as a parent and even begin thinking about baby names, maybe even allow yourself to wander through the baby department in stores, and, even buy a t-shirt or blanket. All of those things will help to allow you to open up the reality that a baby is coming. It may be difficult to do that, but it is important to make an effort and to continue to do so.

Transracial Adoption

Transracial adoption has been and, unfortunately, still is a controversial topic.

My husband and I have 3 beautiful adopted children. We are a "rainbow family." Our oldest son, Jimmy, is Caucasian/Hispanic, our middle son, Charlie, is African American/Korean, and our daughter, Nika, is full African/American. We are privileged to have them and can't imagine our family without them.

Some families feel because of family prejudices, or because they may live in an area where there is little or no diversity, it's best to adopt a child of their own race. I feel in that case, this is probably the best choice.

There is a belief among some, that children of color should be raised only by families that share their culture. There is a valid argument for that belief. However, that option is not always available for them. We have many racially diverse families who have adopted through our office. All of us are in agreement that we are charged with a responsibility to honor the cultures of our children and to educate them in their traditions. We all also believe it's important to provide them access to friends and mentors of their own racial background. This is not an issue any of us takes lightly.

Recently, we saw a documentary about kids in the "system", who had no family available to raise them. There was a girl who was around 11 years old. When she was interviewed, she was asked if she felt it was important that she be raised by an adoptive family of her own race. She looked into the camera and said, "I don't care if my parents are green! I just want to be part of a family and have parents who will love me."

Throughout the years of raising our children, we have believed it very important to introduce them to people and traditions of their own nationalities. We have lived in areas that were somewhat eclectic and multi-racial. We sent them to schools and attended church where most members are of their cultures. We believe it is our responsibility as their family, to encourage them to learn about and participate in events and groups that provide opportunities for relationships with all cultures.

Middle and high school are, under the best circumstances, rampant with bullying and taunting. We've had that experience with all our children.

When there is a racial difference between parents and children, this is often more fuel for the fire. Our kids had difficulties in this area. However, it was not exclusive to race. It seemed to be universal. Hair styles, braces, weight; anything was grounds for teasing and taunting. It was not just about race. They, just as most kids in those age ranges, experienced it all.

It was difficult for us to deal with all of the issues confronting our kids. We became very protective, but always letting them know there would be many different issues with which to deal, throughout their lives. They would always have things to confront. This was the training ground to learn how to deal with whatever came up.

They have flourished, despite their challenges in the area of racial difference, from us. It wasn't always easy for them. Of course, we wish they hadn't had to deal with all the trials, but they're all amazing and we're so proud and grateful to be their parents.

There have been times we've wondered if we have done them a disservice. We wonder if they would have been happier being raised by their biological parents or adoptive parents of their own cultures. We'll never know the answer to that question. However, we do know they're ours and we love them all. We're very grateful to have had them with us and believe they are moving in the direction of being happy, well-rounded adults. In the end, isn't that what all parents want?

What About My Life?

Potential adoptive parents are used to a certain routine and lifestyle that will be seriously impacted by bringing in a baby. Babies pretty much change everything! Waiting parents may feel guilty or selfish when they think of or voice their worries about the changes that will come with bringing a baby into the family.

In spite of their strong desire to have a child, life as they've known it will be over. Those thoughts and feelings are not selfish. They are natural and normal. This is a huge change. But it's important to consciously be aware that this lifestyle change can come with wonderful rewards. This is not an either/or decision. Life takes a major turn when a baby comes in, but eventually, the Sunday morning sleep-in may be interrupted by a little person running in and jumping into the bed to snuggle. The baby becomes the center of everything and lifestyle shifts will become natural.

These fears are part of the process, and can only really be eliminated by discovering personally, how it will all come together. As with many things in life, no matter how much information we may have been given, personal experience is the only way to achieve understanding and certainty.

In fact, one of our families, during their first meeting with me, expressed the fears mentioned above more than once. They are active, travel frequently, and have a busy social life and large extended family. They both had high power jobs. She had made the decision to stay at home if and when they did get a baby. I felt that she was the driving force behind the interest in adoption. He had great concern about losing his/their independence. Both were concerned about the time required caring for an infant. The potential dad, Dan, was so adamant in his worry about these issues, that when they left, I felt he might never be comfortable adopting. At the meeting, he was polite, but reserved. He sat straight upright. At one point, I said, "It's my belief that babies find the families they are supposed to have. I've seen it over and over again." He was kind enough not to roll his eyes, but I got the impression he thought I was a little off. I think I heard something mumbled about "new age claptrap."

Despite it all, it was easy to see how much they cared for each other. He was there because he wanted to investigate in order to honor her desire to adopt.

A few months later, I received a call from a birthmother, Annie, who met all the criteria this couple had mentioned when they interviewed with me. I called them and told them about her. She was due to deliver soon and we needed to find a family quickly.

The potential mom, Maggie, was very interested. She said she would talk with her husband and get back to me. When she did, the conversation revealed that they were "guardedly" interested. We set a meeting between Dan and Maggie and Annie and her parents. Michael and I agreed to meet with all of them in order to break the ice a little. Dan and Maggie were over an hour late. They had traffic problems and called wondering if they should put off the meeting till the next week. I assured them we would all wait and that we should do this now! That time with Annie and her family allowed us to complete the necessary paperwork and to get a strong sense of her feelings about placement. Michael and I felt she was sincere in her wish to place her baby for adoption. When Dan and Maggie arrived they had that "deer in the headlights" look. We stayed about 20 minutes after their arrival, and then left them all alone. During our time there, what almost always happens happened. They discovered many common interests and everyone wanted to go forward. They even discovered that they all had a mutual acquaintance.

When Annie went into labor, the family was there for the delivery. Surprisingly . . . kidding . . . not so surprisingly, this baby was the most beautiful and perfect that had ever been born. It's such a joy to watch adoptive families with their new babies. The love is immediate, natural and complete.

About a week after the baby went home with the family, my phone rang. Maggie sounded frantic. "Nikki, you won't believe what happened!!! This morning I went to the car to go to Starbucks and get coffee. When I started the engine, I realized I had forgotten the baby was in the house. I ran in crying, terrified that I might have actually left him there." "What if I'm not capable of being a good mother? I almost left my baby in the house alone!"

Maggie said she had called Dan and reported this to him. She asked if he thought they should give the baby back. He answered immediately, "You can do this. We are not giving this baby back. He is staying right here! I will do this with or without you!" His parental instincts had kicked in and the reversal was an incredible thing to see. His certainty gave her the strength to know they would be all right.

A few months later Dan and Maggie had a party to honor their baby. They invited us. Dan described how doubtful he had been initially and how he would never have imagined how much he could love a baby. He talked about how he thought what I said to him during our first meeting was pretty much bunk! And, this very tall and strong businessman fought tears as he held his baby son and said, "But now I understand."

He talked about how unexpected his feelings were for this little person who has brought love and joy into their lives…in ways they had never known existed.

Dan is now, not only an amazing daddy, but is doing volunteer work with kids at risk; working on helping them develop their potential and self-esteem.

This is one of my favorite adoption stories. I love hearing about their guy walking and beginning to talk and the wonder they experience with each new developmental milestone. He is over 2 years old now, beautiful and very busy. Adoption is a beautiful journey and it has been pure joy watching this family allow it to unfold.

2.

Getting Started

How To Begin The Process

The dream of adopting a baby is an exciting and romantic one. When it is time to take the first step, other emotions may surface; confusion about how to proceed along with feeling overwhelmed and anxious. The desire for family comes with excitement and joy at the prospect of bringing a baby into your hearts and lives. The wish to complete your family also comes with doubts about whether you have the skills to parent and will do a good job of it. There is the realization that life will drastically change and a little person will now be the focus of everything. While the upcoming change in your life may feel daunting and overwhelming, the good news is the process is much simpler than most people perceive it to be.

When Michael and I began to look into adoption, we had no idea how to begin. A friend told us about an adoption attorney in our area. She said she and her husband had met with him and felt very comfortable. We set an appointment and went to see him. We felt that the anxiety we were feeling was visible and that he would tell us we were too neurotic, too old, too something, to adopt. Aside from all that, certainly no birthmother would ever place her baby with someone who would wear those shoes! We were terrified.

The attorney was very kind and seemed to have experienced this type of illogical fear before. He was reassuring and said he could help us. He asked our requirements for a birthmother and told us since we were open to almost any scenario, he could help us find our baby in a relatively short period of time.

Our lives changed on that day. We went from a couple to a family at that moment…a family waiting for its' new addition. There was a "feeling" that he was coming, and every day the waiting was stressful and difficult, but also exciting. Each day, we tried to remember that if we didn't hear that day, we were one day closer to the day we would.

Choosing Your Professional Representatives

We chose to use an independent adoption attorney for our adoption. Each state has its' own adoption laws and requirements for the legal part of the process. Your adoption professionals will be able to work with you according to what is allowable where you live. It is important to research the differences between agency, independent/private, or county adoptions. If you are working on an independent adoption with an attorney, be sure the attorney specializes in adoption. There are many facets to this process, and an attorney who does not specialize in adoption may not be aware of specific or new laws. Therefore, he may not have the same knowledge and skill in this field. An adoption attorney will have referrals for your home study, and be able to provide information about agencies, and adoption professionals. He can also refer you to attorneys/ agencies in other states; should your baby be born out of your home state. An adoption specific attorney will be able to answer questions others may not. There is a national organization of adoption lawyers; The American Academy of Adoption Attorneys.

Also, in California there is the Academy of California Adoption Lawyers. These organizations can make referrals for attorneys who can help and will meet your individual needs. In addition, these organizations provide referrals of adoption agencies to complete your home study and assist with the legal issues involved with your adoption. Some adoption attorneys and agencies also assist in locating a birthmother.

Be sure, when you choose legal representatives, agency or attorney, they will be available during the baby's delivery and the hospital stay for birthmom and baby. Situations can arise during that time which may require input and assistance from them.

Adoption Agencies

A licensed adoption agency can be an all-in-one option. Agencies will do birthmother counseling, your home study, termination of birthparents' rights, and the legal work on your adoption. It's a good idea to check out all options near you and see what fits best for your individual needs.

Adoption Agency Or Attorney

As stated, an adoption agency for an agency adoption, or adoption attorney for a private/ independent adoption, is necessary to complete the legal work on your adoption. Costs for legal services can vary according to the needs in each individual case. Your agency or attorney will give you basic costs and talk with you about additional expenses pertinent to your case.

Some attorneys and agencies will search for your baby. There are additional fees for this part of the service. Check with your professionals regarding this issue and, if they do provide this service, the costs involved.

Adoption Facilitator

Many states will allow the use of a facilitator to assist and guide you in your efforts to locate the birthmother of your baby. Some do not. It's essential that you check the laws in your state in order to see if this option is a possibility for you.

Having our own adoption facilitation office has offered us an opportunity to participate with families and birthparents and helping them come together. The function of an adoption facilitator is to advertise for and screen potential birthmothers. They will determine the requirements of each family in order to locate a birthmother who will be a good match for them. An important part of the screening process with each birthmother includes questions about her preferences regarding the family who will adopt her baby. At that point, the facilitator will present families to her that have the same criteria.

When she expresses a preference for a family, the facilitator will contact the family and explain the birthmother's situation; and, if, after talking or meeting with each other there is an agreement, the match will go forward from there. Fees for facilitators vary, so if you have an interest in this service, it's a good idea to research which office fits your needs and your budget. Facilitators are not allowed to provide legal services or professional counseling for the adoption. For that, your facilitator can refer you to a licensed counselor; preferably one who specializes in adoption.

Once you have done this, you will want to talk with and meet the people who have been referred to you. As important as it is to find experts who are recommended and who fall within state requirements, it is equally important to find professionals with whom you feel comfortable.

You need to know they are interested in knowing your requirements and what works for your family, when searching for your birthparents and baby. They must be willing to support you, emotionally, through the process. This is a deeply personal experience for all parties involved. Knowing you will have someone to talk with when you have questions, or need support, is a helpful part of the process.

Get the opinions of your professionals regarding posting your presentation on the web. There are differing schools of thought about the benefits of doing so. Should you choose to do so, please do so only with the guidance of your professionals. Attempting to screen a birthmother on your own, especially one that comes from your web posting, is not advisable. Your professionals will be able to get a sense of the birthmother, her circumstances, needs and wishes, and will verify her pregnancy before getting you involved.

The Home Study

All adoptive families are required to complete a Home Study in order to bring an adopted baby/child into their families. Home Study requirements may vary from state to state. A completed home study is critical if you are considering adopting a child from another state. It is unlawful to take a child across state lines without a current home study. The basic process is designed to insure the family is an appropriate candidate to raise an adoptive child. Some of the requirements include, all family members must have or have had within the last year, a physical exam along with a TB test. Each participating parent must fill out a very thorough personal history form and submit it. There are referral forms to be sent to four references; usually two personal and two business, to get their take on your ability to be good parents. Each parent must be fingerprinted and the fingerprints must be cleared by the FBI and Department of Justice. A social worker will be assigned to visit the home to be sure it is a safe and appropriate place for a child.

Subsequent to the completion of the home study, there is a post placement process. Post placement home study includes the social worker coming to your home either once or twice after the birth to see that the baby is growing, developing, and bonding normally. Then the pediatrician will fill out a form acknowledging the same, when the baby is around four months old. It may sound daunting, but is a necessary part of the process, and is, in reality, easier than it sounds. The social worker is on your team and wants all of you to do well. Try to relax and let her visits be a pleasant experience where you can brag about how smart and beautiful your baby is. Cookies and tea are nice gestures.

Birthmother/ Birthparent Adoption

Each office has its' own suggestions or requirements for your presentation to the birthmother. Some will require you to provide a completed "birthmother letter/profile" to their office. They may ask for a number of copies of the original letter. Some offices will assist you in putting the letter together or ask for photos and text, and do it for you. There may be an extra charge if the office puts the letter together, or refers a service that will do it for you. This letter is the tool that will evoke a birthmother's interest in you; so, it should be the best representation possible. Most offices will have a web page and will list your letter on their website, should you so desire.

We have a format we like that has provided good success with birthmothers. We suggest a letter with lots of photos, on 11 x 17 cardstock paper folded in half, so that you have a booklet of 4 pages, 8 ½ x 11, interspersed with photos and text. On the front, it is important to have a 4 x 6 photo of yourself/yourselves that is close (waist up) so she can see your face(s) and eyes. If you have a dog or dogs, most birthmothers, with whom I have worked, like a photo with your dogs. The thing for which the birthmother is looking is a sense of warmth and accessibility.

If you are a couple, she will be looking for the relationship between you. She will want to see that you like each other and are having fun together. With every part of the presentation, warm and fuzzy are the key words. The text content should include a greeting and ending that explains your gratitude to be considered as parent(s) of her baby. It should also acknowledge her strength in making an adoption plan for her baby. The ending should include a sentence about wishing her peace in whatever decision she makes.

The body of your letter should tell her about yourself and your family, your work, extended family, and how excited they all are to welcome a new baby into the family. Also recommended is a brief version of why you are choosing to adopt, and how ready you are to do so. You should also stress that education is important and your commitment to providing a strong educational background for your baby. Fun is another important component. She will want to know that although education is a strong commitment on your part, the baby will also have many activities that will be enjoyable and create a well-rounded adult. For some birthmothers, religious or spiritual beliefs of the family are important. For some, they are not. Hobbies are also a critical part of the letter. Some birthmothers will choose a family based on their interests; especially if they match hers, or include an activity she knows she cannot provide and wants her baby to enjoy. Many birthmothers are particularly interested in travel. They may not have the opportunity to travel and want that for their little one. It is always interesting to see the choices they make. Every time I think I know who she will choose, my arrogance is rewarded by a very logical choice I would never have guessed.

A while ago, a birth couple came into my office and asked for help in placing their baby due to be born within a week or two. They were both concerned birthparents who were sincere in their desire to choose just the right family for their baby.

They went over their interests, educational requirements, and other qualities they would like in the family that would raise their little one. We showed them several families who matched their criteria. After taking some time to evaluate the letters, they called me over to say they had made their choice. When they showed me the letter from the family they had chosen, I asked them what it was about them that made them feel this family would be the right one. The birthfather smiled at the birthmother, and then they looked at me and said "The dad is wearing a Steelers t-shirt and I'm a big fan".

All this shows there is no logical rhyme or reason why families are chosen. It is an internal "gut" decision. Someone just "feels" right. I don't think it was just the Steelers that drew them to that family, but it was a factor. They told me later, they had spent a week in Pennsylvania and thought it was a beautiful place to raise a child. And, the adoptive mother and father looked like kind people, met their educational requirements, had strong family support, etc. And, the Steelers shirt didn't' hurt! That was one I wouldn't have guessed.

Enjoy this part of the process. It is your first step toward adding your precious baby to your family, and this is when it begins to feel real. If you have a bit of a wait, don't get discouraged. Hang in! Your baby will find you!

What Will It Cost?

Beginning the adoption process comes with a fair amount of anxiety and uncertainty. One of the biggest questions is: "How much will it cost?" "Can we afford it?" The money issue is a big one and is fraught with stress and worry. There is no definite way to predict the exact costs involved in any adoption. Based on the costs below, your professionals will want to know your total budget.

They will work with you to find a birthmother whose needs will fit with what you can comfortably spend. They'll also let you know how to best move forward so your adoption is financially doable for you. Please be clear about what financial arrangements are appropriate for you. The professionals will use that information as part of your file, in order to locate a birthmother and to form an adoption plan that will work for all.

Mariette and Ben are a wonderful couple who were very hopeful they would be able to adopt. Money was a definite issue for them and, as a result, they were fearful they may not be able to accomplish their dream. They came in with some strict requirements about the birthmother of their baby. We discussed that issue along with their money concerns. We didn't want them to feel they had to compromise requirements that were really important to them. However, we worked with them a little bit to go through each issue that was creating fear. While discussing those issues, we were able to eliminate some of their biggest concerns. What we found was that well-meaning family and friends had spent a substantial amount of time and energy suggesting they be very careful. The biggest warning was to be wary of a birthmother who...whatever. The list was long and specific. We went through each item and provided a little more info about their concerns. Mariette and Ben, after receiving more information regarding the issues that worried them most, were able to let go of some of their fears. Therefore, they felt much more comfortable being presented to birthmothers they may have not considered otherwise.

In their case, since they were local, we were able to find a baby whose birthmother had delivered, and informed the hospital about her wish to place her baby. We received a call from a hospital asking if we could assist her in finding a family for her baby. This baby was a great match for Mariette and Ben. They went to the hospital and met with the birthmother, Sarah, and took their baby boy home the next day.

Because the baby was already here, and Sarah's medical costs were covered by insurance, they were able to accomplish their dream in a very short time and within their budget.

Many families who think they can't afford to adopt, may be able to make it work within their budgets. Ask advice from professionals. It's worth making an appointment and meeting with a facilitator, attorney or agency. They will be able to let you know whether there are ways to make your dream a reality. More often than not, there's a way to work it out. There are built-in costs with every independent or agency adoption. There are also a range of costs that are not required but that may be needed by your birthmother. However, those costs can vary greatly according to laws from state to state, office to office, and case to case. Ask your chosen adoption professionals to give you an estimate on a range of costs for the process. Discuss your budget and get a clear picture of the costs that work for you and your individual adoption plan before you begin.

Birthmother Expenses

Some states do not allow an adoptive family to pay any expenses for the birthmother. Some are so strict in this requirement that you may not be allowed, even, to buy her a cup of coffee. In other states, birthmothers are allowed to have financial help during the last 3 months of the pregnancy. They may also be entitled to help for a month to 2 months after; dependent on whether the birth is natural or via C-section. These expenses are carefully monitored. In California, birthmothers are allowed help with rent, food, clothing, utilities, along with some other specifics. It's critical to check with your agency or attorney to determine your ability to assist your birthmother financially. If you are allowed, legally, to assist her, your professionals will let you know the needs of the individual birthmother. You can determine whether they fit into the financial part of your adoption plan. Some birthmothers may live at home and may need no financial help. Others may need all allowable. Your attorney may have a trust account that will allow you to deposit birthmother expenses and from which they will be paid.

Travel

If your birthmother is out-of-state or is not local, you will be required to travel to her location at least once, to pick up your baby. It's also a good idea, if there is a period of time between match and birth, to take a trip to visit her for a day or two.

It is helpful for you to meet her and any members of her family she may want you to meet as well as the birthfather, if she's comfortable with that. We feel it's helpful to have this opportunity to get to know each other a bit. It helps her to feel more peaceful about the family who will parent her baby.

Medical

Most states allow the adoptive family to pay medical costs. If your birthmother is on Medi-caid or Medi-cal, there will, most likely, be little or no cost to the adoptive family for medical care. If she's not, she may be covered by private insurance. In that case, there will probably be some co-pay expense. Some birthmothers have no insurance, and if that's the case, the adoptive family may be responsible for all medical costs. It's the choice of the family whether they are prepared or willing to pay those expenses. If not, your professionals will look for a birthmother who has some kind of insurance.

Separate Attorney For Birthmother

In California, a birthmother is allowed to have her own attorney, separate from the attorney representing the adoptive family. If she wants her own legal representative, the family is responsible for those fees, up to a certain limit.

Most birthmothers work with the same attorney who represents the family. In the event there is a dispute between birthmother and adoptive family, which cannot be resolved by the attorney for the adoptive family, separate counsel will need to be obtained for the birthmother.

Discuss your budget with your professionals so they can give you guidance on what situations will work the best for you. Don't be afraid to get advice. You may, and likely can, be pleasantly surprised.

3.

Locating The Right Birthmother

Every family, when they begin to think about having children, dreams about how it will be to be parents. What kind of personality will the baby have? What or who will he look like? Will he be a genius, athletic, have a good sense of humor? Of course, he'll be the most beautiful, talented and intelligent child ever born. The assumption is that Mensa is just waiting for him.

When there has been a period of time where no pregnancy has occurred, the option of infertility treatment is usually the next step. After a number of treatments with no results, the question comes up whether to continue along that path. At the time, there is a realization that they may be unable to conceive and deliver a biological child, a shift occurs. It's a very emotional time and our experience with our families has included descriptions of grief and depression. After giving themselves time to process, they may begin to look at alternative options.

For example, one of our families told us they had a difficult time deciding to move forward in researching adoption. They said they felt committing to adoption meant committing to letting go of the dream of conceiving their own children. It was very emotional for them and took some time to process.

When looking into adopting, a new series of worries will come up. Now it's wondering whether or not they'll be successful, how hard it will be to do it, how long it will take and what it will cost. Along with that is the realization that the baby will not share any genetic components with them. They can't count on the baby having Daddy's thick hair and beautiful brown eyes, or a cleft in his chin like Uncle Harry. If it's a girl she won't inherit Grandma's gift of dance or her amazing artistic ability.

And on the flip side, what kind of genes will the baby inherit? Will she be pretty, smart, healthy? Although they're aware they can't control who the baby would be that they would deliver biologically, there would probably be some "known's" they could count on. It's a very difficult realization that they can't continue the family line, but add to that the uncertainty of who any child they adopt will be, and it's a lot to handle. With adoption, all bets are off. They can't control anything. They can't have any knowledge of who this little person will be, and it can be terrifying.

We had an opportunity to share a dinner, many years ago when our boys were small, with a talk radio personality. He's a strong advocate for adoption. He and his wife also had a small adopted son, and wanted to know more about our office and our family. He told us that when he and his wife had been dealing with infertility, they began discussing adoption. He said, "I was concerned about what kind of genes an adopted baby would have."

Then, he said, "But then I started to think based on what I know about the genetic factors in my own family, adoption might be better. Now that we have our son, we can see we hit the jackpot."

After researching adoption professionals and choosing which one is the best fit for you, there will be a conversation about what qualities you are looking for in the birthmother of your baby. Many families will start this process proclaiming a desire for a birthmother who will look just like them, who is a college student with straight A's." It's important to remember that, although you are certainly encouraged and able to make whatever requests are important to you, be aware that the more specific you are, the longer it may take to locate a match. And, if your specifications are rigid, you may miss a wonderful opportunity. Whatever requirements you have are fine, just be aware that the more areas in which you can be flexible, the faster you may find a situation that is right for you.

In our experience, the gender issue is the strongest evidence of this. Some offices are not comfortable working with a family who will only accept a specific gender. We are very willing to accommodate that desire, but always inform our families that this requirement adds time because the majority of birthmothers don't know the gender of their babies when they come to us. Of the ones who do, half are having the other sex; so it substantially limits the number of birthmothers to whom they can be presented.

Specific requirements are okay. This is a baby you will raise and to whom you will have a lifetime commitment. You are the only people who know what's right for your family. However, in an attempt to really confuse you, always remember that sometimes the biggest miracles in your lives come in completely different packages than you imagined. Try to be as open as you can be, maybe a bit out of your comfort zone.

The more adoptions we have had the privilege of working, the more we've seen and are firmly convinced you'll get the right one. I know that sounds hokey, but we've seen it over and over again. My clients will certainly testify to that. Interestingly, each of our families has the cutest, smartest, and most talented child ever born.

4.

Waiting

How Long Will We Have To Wait For A Match?

Many families have told me waiting is the most difficult part of the process. Getting to the adoption process has taken whatever time it has taken. Usually families who have been through the infertility process, and decided to move on to adoption, feel as though they want it yesterday. That's certainly understandable. When they are ready, their first step is to research and find the professionals that feel right for them.

After signing on with the appropriate adoption professionals, they will most likely be instructed to gather photos, and write text about their lives and reasons for wanting to adopt. The letter will contain pertinent information they want to share with a potential birthmother. Some families will want to do this on their own; following whatever format is used in the agency/attorney or facilitator's office. Some offices will offer options to have it done for them.

This presentation is the most critical part of their introduction to the birthmother. They have put in a great deal of heart and thought to make it the best representation they can. The photos and text will give her a snapshot of the family, home, hobbies, travels, as well as an expression of what it means to form or add to their family through adoption.

Many families have specific criteria, race or gender requirements and a preferred timeline, usually immediate. Some have drug and alcohol restrictions; all normal and all reasonable. Whatever the family's requirements, in most cases, they are doable. However, if your wishes are really specific, significant criteria can add to your wait.

The impatience and desire to find the right birthparents and baby are understandable; especially because this is an area where again, they have no control.

No one can tell them who this person is, or when she will show up. After what they have been through, this is sometimes overwhelming and frustrating and feels impossible to deal with.

We have many stories of families who were on the verge of quitting and with some gentle nudging to hold on, have gone on to adopt their babies. It is most important not to give up. We have lots of families who can testify to that.

Can We Shorten The Wait?

As I said, most families feel they've done all the waiting they need to do. The lack of control in this area is particularly hard and it's completely understandable that the family can get frustrated.

In the case where there has been a wait of considerable length, something to consider might be to revise your profile or birthmother presentation. It's also a good idea to decide whether you can ease some of your requirements. If you can do that comfortably, it can lessen the wait. Sometimes a small change can make a big difference.

It's critical, especially at this time, to feel comfortable with and trust your adoption professionals. It's easy to want to lay blame on the people who appear to be responsible for not having found the birthmother and baby you've been wanting for so long. Of course, on some level you're aware that this anger is not really aimed there. It has to be someone's responsibility that this isn't happening. You just want to be parents.

It's important to remember that your adoption professionals can talk with potential birthmothers about you and show your profile to them, but cannot, legally or in any way, tell or even suggest that a birthmother should choose a specific family. This is, no doubt, one of the most important decisions she will ever make, and it has to be the right one for her and her baby. She has to feel peaceful about where and with whom her baby will be raised.

It's never personal if a birthmother chooses another family. It's just what's right for her, and what she believes is best for her baby. Just as you have criteria with regard to the qualities, lifestyle, medical issues, race and/or gender of the baby, etc., she also has requirements concerning the family who will raise her baby. Our goal and our job, as with all adoption professionals who are assisting birthmothers and families in forming an adoption plan, is to be as clear as possible in the knowledge of what each of the parties is requiring.

Something else to think about is whether your criteria is so rigid that it may be keeping you from being presented to birthmothers who might be a good match for you. You might think about looking, once more, at your requirements and defining whether you might be able to widen the scope of what you've requested. Someone once told me that it's very possible the perfect mate/job/baby may not meet the pictures you've set for yourself. I've seen evidence of that in our own family; and after reflecting about it, feel we got the perfect ones. They didn't match our ideas of them, but they're definitely ours.

We have many examples of families who came into the office with a list. After waiting a while and re-examining that list a few months later, have let go of some of their restrictions and been very happily surprised that the baby they adopt couldn't be more perfect. Interestingly, they matched very few of the strict criteria they initially requested.

Norm and Gina came in with a list of 11 requirements, including religion, nationality, hair and eye color, gender, birthfather involvement and so on. They were certain all these requirements must be met. We let them know it was unlikely we would find a birthmother who matched, completely, what they were asking, in a timely manner. In essence, they wanted the "perfect" baby. We assured them biological children rarely match the exact picture the parents have imagined, and still, to the parents, their baby is the most wonderful child ever born. They said they understood, but these conditions were important to them. We felt, at that time, they were set, and told them we would move forward according to what they were requesting.

A few months later we met again, and they relaxed a few of their restrictions. They were matched 3 months later and adopted their "perfect" baby. He met only 2 of the original conditions they gave us.

Try to remember, during the wait, your baby is out there and you will find each other. Hang in! It will happen!

5.

Birthmothers/ Birthparents: Fear And Gratitude

"BIRTHMOTHER"…a word that strikes fear in the hearts of even the hardiest of potential adoptive parents. The media coverage and word of mouth stories describe and embellish stories of women who are not actually pregnant, or women who are working with 7 families at a time, or who take money from innocent families having no intention of placing their babies. The other possibility is that they are drug addicts, who take adoptive parents' money and use it to supply their habits. It is rare to see any media about the tens of thousands of positive adoption stories that take place in this country each year.

A few years ago, I received a call from one of the tabloid shows asking if I had any good adoption scam stories. I told them I did not, but that I had over 150 stories that were really great. They declined and hung up.

This is a real shame. The truth is, the vast majority of birthmothers are courageous women who love their babies. They are making difficult and brave choices for their little ones that require enormous strength and selflessness. Those of us who are blessed to be adoptive parents, and have known our birthmothers/birthfathers, feel grateful for that opportunity. It's a blessing to have had the opportunity to have information about our little ones' roots.

The truth is most birthmothers form adoption plans for their babies because they are not in a position to raise a child. The difficulty of allowing her child to be raised by another family is beyond description.

An important and critical thing to remember is these women are going through a difficult time in their lives. Many of them are in dire circumstances. Often, it's uncomfortable for adoptive parents to look at the extreme poverty she may be experiencing, or her life raising 4 other young children with no emotional or financial support.

One of our recent birthmothers contacted us during her hospital stay and wanted to place her new baby daughter for adoption. I met with her, showed her some families and completed all the necessary paperwork. She chose a family who came to the hospital immediately. They formed an instant bond and all the necessary legal work for that part of the process was completed. She asked for no financial help.

The social worker took her home from the hospital after the adoptive family left with the baby. The worker called me after she left her; to tell me her living circumstances were heartbreaking. She, her mother and 1-year-old son were living in a garage with no heat or air conditioning. It was the hottest time of the year. They clearly needed food, diapers, and other necessities that we take for granted. The family was able to help her with the basics like food, supplies for her toddler and other items to assist her to provide what was needed for her family's well-being. In this case, as in most, the placement of her baby took incredible courage and strength, and the desire to provide a better life for her and her son. She never mentioned her living conditions or her extreme need. We were happy to have discovered a way to help her.

Sometimes birthmothers may seem a little hostile or even offensive. This is most often a defense mechanism. She may be upset about being in the position of not being able to keep her baby, and, or, somewhat jealous of the adoptive mother because she can give the baby what the birthmother cannot. Underneath, they are usually grateful for the life the family will be giving their babies. They just don't know how to show it.

If you are involved with a match with a birthmother who may be somewhat difficult, please think about her life conditions. Sometimes a little compassion can go a long way.

There are also cases where adoptive parents, out of fear, may be hostile to the idea of meeting or getting to know a birthmother. "Do we have to meet her?" There have been times when it's been difficult for me not to have judgment on that attitude. But, and it's a big but, I try to remember how fearful I was of losing our baby either before birth or after until the birthmother's rights had been terminated. If you have these feelings, please share them with a counselor and/or your adoption professionals. They will be able to help you process them, so that you can move on to have a positive relationship with your birthmother. I don't think I'm alone in remembering moments of wishing we could just have the baby delivered to our doorstep. You'll find you're not alone, but it's important to move through to the other side of these feelings. Had we held on to them, we would have missed some wonderful times learning about our baby's heredity, possible personality, and physical traits. There is much to learn from and appreciate about your birthmother. Any time you can spend getting to know about her is of benefit to your baby. Eventually, there will be questions like, "Who do I look like?", "Why do I love to ride horses?" If you know and can share the answers to these questions in a way that is natural, it will make your child more secure in his/her identity.

I think this is most important in families where there may already be biological children. Adopted children will likely feel "different" and that "they don't fit". When you can say, "Your birthmother loved the outdoors and was very interested in horses" they gain an understanding of the part of them that's their roots. That helps them to develop an understanding of that part of who they are. Information about their roots can only boost their self-esteem.

The truth is, most birthmothers motives are selfless and for the benefit of their babies. Remember the sacrifice and strength required for a birthmother to form and complete an adoption plan for her baby.

If you feel something is off or your birthmother's attitudes or behavior change in a dramatic way, always report this to your adoption professionals. They will get involved and will work with you to determine if these changes are serious, and, if so, what can be done to assist.

If there is a major issue, they will let you know if or when they feel it may be risky to continue. Value their guidance. They are there to support you. Use them.

Most of the time, issues are easily resolved, but if this is questionable, listen and respond accordingly. It's very important to remember that if these women were stable at this time, we wouldn't be hearing from them. They need and deserve our compassion and gratitude.

Enjoy your time with your birthmother. It's irreplaceable.

6.

Birthmother Screening

How Is She Screened?

The process of screening the birthmother covers areas pertinent to her emotional commitment to the adoption process, as well as an overview of the legal issues required to complete the adoption plan.

The first and most important information we can give you about screening is NEVER do it on your own. Potential adoptive parents can miss signals or red flags in their excitement about talking with a birthmother who may choose them. Always work with an adoption professional. Let them know your wishes and desires for the baby you wish to adopt…what you want and what you don't want. An adoption professional can screen without the emotional attachment that a potential family cannot help feeling.

Most of the time, birthmothers are sincere in their wish to place a baby and are honest people with high integrity. However, there are times when this is not the case and it is much easier to catch these situations when a professional is involved. There are certain language patterns and signals that can give us a sense of possible drug use and/or insincerity. Listening to the birthmother's tone and needs during the first contact, can give us a strong sense of her.

Over the years, we have had several calls from supposed birthfathers/birthmothers claiming to be in a stressful and serious situation, usually homeless, possibly living in a car, pregnant and nowhere to go. They need immediate financial help. Most often, the due date given is several months away. These callers may sound sincere and their stories sound real. However, when pressed to provide the necessary proof of pregnancy or completed paperwork, there is always a reason it can't happen.

Sometimes, they will say there is no way for me to get the paperwork to them. They may say they don't have an address or there is no copy store where I can fax it. However, these same people will always be near a Western Union or somewhere that money can be wired. At that point, we inform them we can go no further.

Even after my years working in adoption, a few months ago I was almost caught up in one of these situations. We received a call from a man who said his wife was pregnant and due in 3 months. They were on the east coast. They had lost their home and he had lost his job. They were living in their van. They wanted to drive to California where he would find a job and housing for them. Initially, they asked for nothing. On the second call, they said they would need traveling money. I told them I would need a current proof of pregnancy (that day), he said they would get and fax it to me. They provided me with the fax number of a local printer, and I faxed them the necessary paperwork to get started. They immediately filled it out and faxed it right back. Their immediate response to that request was encouraging. I contacted one of our attorneys about how to work with the financial need to get here. (I don't usually work with out-of-state birthmothers, so I wanted to be sure I was responding correctly and in accordance with California law.) His suggestion was to verify the proof-of-pregnancy, then provide enough money to get them part of the way here. At the point they arrived in, maybe Denver, we could wire the balance of the money needed to get them the rest of the way to Los Angeles, where we would meet at his office, complete the rest of the necessary paperwork, and begin the match process.

Over the course of the next day or two, we contacted a couple of families that matched the criteria they had given me. I informed them of the risks involved in this type of situation. One of them was willing to speak with the birthparents.

They spoke and all involved seemed happy with each other and willing to consider meeting upon their arrival toward a possible match. They did fax me the proof of pregnancy. The appearance of it was not what we normally see and made me somewhat suspicious. It was plain paper with just the name, address and phone number of the clinic typed on it. There was a typed note verifying that this woman was pregnant and a due date, with a scribbled signature, supposedly by a doctor.

Normally, there is more identifying information about the doctor and the clinic, as well as license numbers for both. By the time I received the proof, it was after business hours back east. Since I wanted to verify the veracity of the proof, I told the birthmother when she called to see if we had received it, that it came from the fax machine blurry. She immediately offered to re-fax it. I told her I would just call the clinic in the morning and ask them to send it. She got off the phone quickly and said they would call me back in the morning. I never heard from them again. The following morning I called the clinic. They said they had never heard of her and faxed me their actual proof form, which was completely different.

While I was always wary of this couple, the thing that hooked me, initially, was that the birthfather sounded real and very sincere. He said all the right things. He was clear he wanted to support his own family. He simply wanted help getting here and would immediately begin a job search and search for a place to live. Although they would need support until he was able to accomplish that, he was adamant he knew and was serious about his obligation to their well-being. He also had the standard patter down about wanting this baby to have a stable life that they were not able to provide.

As my suspicions grew, I knew we would not want our family to get involved, or to provide any money at that point. Letting the birthmother know we were going to talk with the clinic was the defining moment. She obviously would not have been afraid for me to have that conversation, had she been legitimate.

It is difficult to hear a family who seems to be in serious need without responding. A potential adoptive family is more likely to want to help without the necessary backup information. That is a natural and compassionate response. That is why, if the family receives a call from a possible birthmother, their first response should be to contact their adoption professional and allow them to do the screening. If they have not yet hired a professional, that moment is the moment to do it. Unfortunately, these stories are not unusual among birthparents that are looking for cash without the intention to place the baby, if there is a baby. Again, please remember this is not a common occurrence. Most birthmothers are legitimate and only want to give their babies a good life. That is why they consider adoption.

However, these kinds of scams are out there. For that reason, arming yourselves with a good professional can enhance your chances of finding the right birthmother faster. And, in a case like this, that can save a lot of heartache.

Our Screening Process

Our office talks with each birthmother about 5 specific issues.

Level Of Certainty And Commitment To Forming An Adoption Plan

Our first question to any birthmother is how sure she is about placing her baby. I like to work with birthmothers in Southern California, if possible, so that we can meet and I can spend time getting to know her and her reasons for considering adoption. I also want to look at her energy, eye contact, and body language while we are discussing this. Placing a baby for adoption is one of the most difficult choices any woman has to face. Many times, these are young girls who are not prepared to make a decision of this scope, and yet they must. We feel it is essential to be available, understanding and compassionate, but also need to be as certain as we can, before matching her with a family that she is as committed as possible, at this point, to following through.

No birthmother can predict 100%, during the pregnancy, her ability to follow through with placement after the birth. For this reason, it is important that she be as clear as possible when forming the adoption plan during the screening process. During this phase, eye contact is very important. If she is looking away and tells me she is 95% certain, that is a big concern. Ninety-five percent, when you have just delivered a baby and the baby is in the room, and hormones are working overtime, is not a good percentage. When the baby is a reality, letting go is extremely difficult for most birthmothers; young ones in particular. It is at this point that earlier clarity is most helpful.

Of course, regardless of her commitment to the process during her pregnancy, that can change at any time, especially during the hospital stay after the birth. If she expresses doubt and uncertainty during the screening process, it may be best to wait until the birth to match. If she wishes to place at that time, it is more likely the placement will proceed.

In cases where this feels like the appropriate direction, there are indications that earlier matching may place more stress and pressure on the birthmother. That can result in resentment and more likelihood that the adoption plan may ultimately fail. When that happens, the birthmother may experience guilt and doubt and the family is heartbroken.

The other possibility is to go forward with the match, if the birthmother wishes to do so. Some birthmothers feel the need to meet and get to know the family who will adopt their babies before they make a firm commitment to the adoption plan. When the family understands that there is ambivalence, and the possibility of her changing her mind is stronger than average, they can make the decision whether or not to go forward knowing the risk. In some cases, once the birthmother knows the family, she will often relax and feel more peaceful about her decision to place. As with everything else, each birthmother is unique, as is each family.

All birthmothers are offered counseling during this time, with a licensed therapist or counselor, to assist them in understanding the adoption process and the grief and loss that may accompany the placement of the baby. We always urge them to avail themselves of this service. Often the counselors will assist them in making a list of the reasons for the adoption decision. The list is helpful, after the birth, in affirming that the circumstances that led to the decision to place, generally, have not changed.

We always let our birthmothers know that grieving is a normal part of the process, and it does not mean she has made a mistake. It is just something that goes with letting go of the baby. Some of our former birthmothers will talk with women in the process of placing to reassure them and help them achieve clarity and, hopefully, peace.

All of our birthmothers are reassured that no one in our office or any of our associates will coerce or pressure them into placing a baby for adoption. That is a deeply personal decision, and while we can give information, a decision of this magnitude must, finally, be made by the birthmother. Whatever her decision, it is hers alone and must be respected by all involved.

We tell our birthmothers that whatever decision they make, it is important to surround themselves with family and/or friends who will support that decision.

It is not productive to allow pressure from people who disagree and/or want to push for their own desired result.

Recently, we had a case where a very young birthmother discovered her pregnancy only when she was close to 7 months pregnant. She told her mother and they began to sort out possibilities. The birthmother decided on adoption. She wanted to get back to her life and felt she was not ready for the responsibilities attached with being a mom at 16. The birthfather, a little younger, was also in favor of placing the baby, as was his family.

Birthmom's mother and father were in shock and wanted to be sure she was making the decision to place for the right reasons. Her mother was not really in favor of an adoption plan and was willing to and interested in keeping the baby. I asked the mother if she felt she could truly support her daughter's decision should she choose to place. I told her that, more than anyone else, her daughter would need her unconditional support during the time after placement, and she needed to be willing to be completely there for her should she decide to go forward. She said she thought she could. There was a lot of discussion between all in the family and, they remained reticent to choose a family for the baby.

Ultimately, we felt it was best they wait to make a firm decision until the baby was born. If adoption was the desired plan at that time, we would have birthmom choose a family and get them there immediately.

We felt that to do so before would create cause for the birthmother to feel pressured into an action for which she was not ready. In this case, although the birthmother feels adoption is the best option for her and for the baby, she is 16, and if there is family pressure at the hospital, especially after she has seen the baby, she may be unable to continue with her plan to place. With regard to the potential family, meeting and getting to know her will create a strong bond and connection to the birthmother and the baby, and we are careful not to put a family in that position unless we feel as sure as we can at this moment, the birthmother is likely to follow through.

It is not a common occurrence, for a birthmother to change her mind during the pregnancy or just after the birth, but with a very young woman, it is important to give her the opportunity and time to be as clear as she can. In this case, if the choice is to place, the placement has a much better chance to go forward to completion if it comes from clarity and having an opportunity to feel peaceful about her choice.

Birthfather Involvement

As a facilitator, our responsibility with regard to the birthfather is to assess his status and involvement during our interview with the birthmother. Once that has been accomplished, all information regarding legal requirements is turned over to the attorney and/or agency involved in the case. We will discuss with the birthmother, the father's position regarding her pregnancy and the adoption option. We refer him to the legal representative so that the appropriate action can be taken to terminate his parental rights.

Are she and the baby's father married, and/or living together?

If so, do they have children together?

Is he a steady boyfriend, or a casual relationship?

Is he involved with the pregnancy, assisting financially and emotionally?

Was it a one-night involvement? If so, can she provide his name and information?

Was this pregnancy the result of a consensual event?   ♥

Many people believe the birthfather must consent in all cases. That is not accurate. There are specific laws about his legal involvement. Your attorney/agency will know the legal requirements in your state and will inform you about what is needed and the likelihood that these requirements can be met in your individual case.

Our belief is that it is, for many reasons, a benefit to have birthfather involvement in the pregnancy and the adoption plan. First, if this is a strong relationship, his emotional support is important during this stressful time. And, the ability to get a medical profile from both birthparents is of great value.

When the birthfather is involved, it is a wonderful opportunity for the adoptive family to learn about his interests, his beliefs, talents and goals. Often, birthfathers have difficulty coping with the reality that, at this time, they are unable to provide for the addition of a child. It is difficult for them and they may feel like they are failing their families.

When that is the case, it is beneficial, especially, for the adoptive father to talk with him. It's helpful to let him know how grateful you are for his participation

in the birth of the baby and your adoption. He needs
to feel that you are including him, that you value his
input and opinions, and that you are concerned about
his feelings. He will be feeling grief and loss, as is the
birthmother, but his emotions and concerns are rarely
considered.

He will usually feel it is his job to support and
console her and that his own feelings need to be put
aside. For this reason, it is helpful and important
to let him know you consider him an integral part
of the adoption plan. If there are some issues that
would make the birthmother uncomfortable having
the birthfather present, then those issues should be
discussed prior to her hospital confinement.

In California, legally there are two types of
birthfathers...presumed and alleged. A presumed
father is a husband or a live-in boyfriend, who has
acknowledged paternity of this baby, and who is
actively involved in the emotional and financial
support of the birthmother. His rights are equal to the
birthmother's and he must consent to the adoption. If
a birthmother tells us she is married, that her husband
is the baby's father and he will not consent to the
adoption, we can go no further with her toward an
adoption plan. If he is in agreement, your attorney or

agency will be able to give you specific information on how they will work with him to terminate his parental rights.

A few years ago, we had a call from a birthmother who had 2 little boys, one 2 ½ and the other 18 months. She was expecting twin boys within 2 months. She and the birthfather were separated, but still married. He lived elsewhere and would come to visit the boys every week to 2 weeks for a couple of hours. She was exhausted from caring for the 2 boys by herself, and the pregnancy added to that. She was terrified at the prospect of having 2 more in a short while. She was very clear that placing the twins for adoption was the best option for all 4 children. However, her husband was clear he would not permit the adoption to go through and would not sign any kind of consent to allow her to place. In that case, there was no way we could help her. She was devastated by his decision, but was forced to bring her 2 new baby boys home to a 2-bedroom apartment with no help to care for them or her other 2 boys.

We have had many successful placements where both husband and wife were in agreement. Obviously, that is an optimal situation and we are always thrilled to see the partnership between the birthparents in forming an adoption plan for their baby.

An alleged father may be a casual boyfriend, one-night-stand, friend or the perpetrator of a rape; anyone who is not actively involved with the birthmother and the pregnancy. Obviously, if the pregnancy is the result of a proven rape, there are no birthfather rights. If the birthfather is one of any of the other above-mentioned examples, he can do one of three things: he may sign a denial of paternity if he doesn't believe he is the baby's father; he may sign a waiver which states he knows he has been named as a possible father of the baby, and has been informed of the adoption plan and has no objection; or he may not wish to be involved; in which case, there are options by which his rights can be terminated without his consent. He can be served with notice that he has 30 days after the service or after the birth of the baby, whichever is later. If he comes forward during that time, he must prove fitness and paternity if he wishes to contest the adoption. If he is unavailable or uninterested in participating in any way, the attorney/agency will publish notice in an established newspaper. If he does not respond within the time frame allowed, his rights are automatically terminated. Please consult your legal representatives in order to get more information about the termination of rights for the birthfather.

When we adopted our third child, our daughter Nika, our experience included all 3 types of termination of birthfather's rights. Our birthmother was married to a man who was in jail and could not have been the baby's biological father. However, because they were married, his rights had to be terminated and he had to sign to allow the adoption to go forward.

The man she believed to be the father was in the Service out of the country. He was willing to sign the waiver and we sent it by overnight mail. He signed it with a notary and sent it back overnight.

The third was a man she told us about after our daughter's birth. We did not know how to contact him, so the attorney published for 4 weeks and his rights were terminated.

We would have been very happy to just explain this to our clients without having had to experience it; and it came with no shortage of emotional stress and worry, but all worked well and we consider our daughter 3 times more than normally, ours.

People often have more concern about the birthfather than about the birthmother. That might be because he is generally not involved. So, he becomes an unknown. Whatever the situation, your legal representatives will advise you on whether what is known about him warrants moving forward with your adoption plan.

We always love to have birthfather involvement. In my experience, that is not the case most of the time. Also, in my experience, this is not usually a deal breaker. If your legal rep feels this is a doable situation, and his rights can be effectively terminated, that is a good indication it is safe to move forward. We had no active involvement from any of the birthfathers of our children and we have had 3 happy and successful adoptions. Use your instincts, but trust in the professionals. They have had experience in all aspects of determining the risks involved, and they are not emotionally involved. Don't be afraid of the birthfather. In the vast majority of cases, his situation is assessed and addressed without complication.

Family Support For The Adoption Plan

The experience of placing a baby for adoption is always, understandably, stressful and emotionally difficult. As a result, there is a need for emotional support. In most cases, family agreement and willingness to be there is very helpful, especially if the birthmother is young. With a young birthmother, support from her mother is especially important. A teen who is pregnant does not need the consent of her parents to place a baby, and her parents have no legal rights to the baby, or to forbid her to place. However, Mom is Mom, and Mom has influence. For that reason, we need to understand what her family situation is with regard to her adoption plan.

We have had cases where family support is there and where there is opposition from the family. The results are usually predictable in both situations.

One of our birthmothers, Carolyn, was very young, just 14, and about a month prior to her due date, her mother, Diane, brought her to our office. Diane wanted, very much, for Carolyn to place her baby with a wonderful family who would give the baby the love and guidance he would need. I took Carolyn aside, independent of her mother, and asked her, "Are you sure this is what you want? I know your mother wants this for you, but how do you feel?" She said, "This is my wish for my baby. I want him to have a good life with all the financial support and life experiences I can't give him now. I want to know he will go to college." We completed the necessary paperwork and showed her letters from potential families. She chose a family with whom she felt an immediate connection. A few weeks later the baby was born, and the family, Don and Belle, who lived out of state, flew in and spent the hospital time with Carolyn and Diane.

I spoke with Belle recently, and she told me they are in contact with Carolyn and Diane, and all is going well. Carolyn has gone on to get her education and is flourishing. She is finishing college and is engaged.

Of course, there are exceptions to every rule and I have worked with many birthmothers who have told me their families were not excited about or supportive of adoption, who have then gone on to have successful placements.

One of our birthmothers, Clare who was also a teen, was clear she wasn't ready to parent. Her mother was vehemently opposed to the placement of the baby. This was a great concern to all of us, especially to the adoptive parents she had chosen, Neil and Patty. I think, because of her relationship with Neil and Patty, Clare was able to move forward and she placed her baby with them. A few months later, Clare suddenly suffered a stroke. Her mother called and asked us to contact the adoptive parents of the baby and let them know. There was no way to know the outcome for Clare and, despite her opposition to the adoption; her mother felt they should be advised. Neil was a pilot with a major airline and Patty was a flight attendant. When I reached them, they took the next available flight out. They spent 3 days in the hospital with Clare, talking about and showing her photos of the baby. They took shifts with her mother so that someone was with her at all times. As she improved, the doctors said they felt that Neil and Patty's presence had assisted in her recovery. Clare is fully recovered, and has since married and has 2 more children. This is an important example of the benefits of a close relationship between birthmother and adoptive family. The bond between a birthmom and adoptive mom can be very powerful.

We can never predict the outcome of any adoption plan, with respect to family support, and for this reason, we feel it is necessary to have as much information about the birthmother's wishes and her relationships with the people in her immediate support system. One major point we want to explore is, if she truly believes adoption is the right choice, does she have the ability to move forward in the face of disagreement from the people around her? No one in our office will, for any reason, attempt to influence the decision of any birthmother. However, if she is clear about her choice, either way, we suggest she look for support from the people who will be fully behind her decision.

Every birthmother has a different story. Her first obligation to herself and her baby is to find clarity in her decision, whatever it is, and to move forward with the plan that gives her peace in her own heart.

Health

With all areas of the screening process, we are careful to listen closely to the answers to our questions. We need to get a sense of the birthmother's needs and wishes, as well as her commitment to the adoption process. Birthmother's and baby's health is one of the most significant areas of the screening process. This is especially true because the health history of the pregnancy and the birthmother is critical to the adoption process and to finding the right family for the baby. The questions she will be asked are:

How is she feeling? Are there any complications in the pregnancy so far?

Has she been getting prenatal care? If so, when did it begin and has she been going to the doctor on a regular basis?

What is the contact information for her doctor?

Has she been given a due date?

Has she had an ultrasound or amniocentesis?

(Amniocentesis not usually done unless there is a medical reason). If it is done, there is a time frame that is ideal for this procedure. There are screening tests that are done for pregnant women and you should check with your own Gynecologist and her Obstetrician to determine what tests need to be done and the timing involved.

Does she know the gender of her baby?

Some birthmothers have had ultrasounds and have knowledge of the gender of the baby prior to contacting us or getting matched with a family. And, with a baby that has been born, of course, we will know the gender at the time of contacting the family regarding a match with this particular birthmother and baby. If a family has a specific gender preference, and are matching with a birthmother who has not yet given birth, we generally don't present that family to a birthmother who has not had testing to confirm gender.

Does she have health insurance or medi-cal/ medic-aid?

If she has her own insurance does she have a co-pay? If so, the adoptive family will be responsible for the co-pay. If she has no insurance the adoptive family will be responsible for her medical care. We need to know this information so that, if medical bills need to be paid by the family, we can find a family who is able to and comfortable paying those expenses.

Does she know where she will deliver?

This is important because, while some hospitals are "adoption-friendly", some are not. It is important to know this. In this way, we can determine whether we should have her talk with her doctor about changing hospitals if the initial hospital will not be supportive of her adoption plan. The hospital stay is a critical time for birthmom and it is imperative that she is emotionally supported, not just by family, and the adoptive family, but by the hospital staff, as well. On a few occasions nurses have come into the room at night, when the birthmother is sleeping, and, at her most vulnerable, and made comments like: "Oh, honey, your baby is so pretty, why do you want to give her to someone else? You can do it." Or, "You're giving away your baby? Why don't you just throw her in the trash?"

I've never heard of any hospital that will allow this behavior. For that reason, it's important to know the hospital's general philosophy regarding adoption.

Of course, we want to be as sure as we can that this won't happen. These nurses have no idea that these women are, or their circumstances; they each have their own agenda about adoption. Especially, with a young birthmother, this can create extreme upset or even doubt and uncertainty about her adoption choice. We try to prepare our birthmothers for this possibility by suggesting, should someone come in and attempt to sabotage her adoption plan, that she get the name of the person and ask her to leave immediately. Then this should be reported to her doctor, or the attorney, social worker, or to us.

In an effort to avoid this, we suggest that someone stay with the birthmother at night, during her hospital stay. If the birthmother wants her mom, or the father of the baby, or the adoptive mom to be with her, that situation is unlikely to occur.

If birthmom is interested in having the adoptive mom stay with her, this is often the ideal scene. It gives them a chance to bond and learn more about each other in a quiet setting; and, of course the time of sharing care of the baby is precious and invaluable.

How much prenatal care has she received?

Of course, we all want to know that the birthmother of our baby has been getting medical care from the beginning of her pregnancy. Although this is often the case, it is not always true. If the birthmother comes to us during her pregnancy and has not had care, we will work with the adoptive family to help her find a doctor and get started. One of the forms each birthmother signs for us is an authorization for release of all medical records for the pregnancy, birth, and hospital for her and the baby. She also signs a release to be tested for AIDS, drugs and alcohol. If this has not already happened we have it done as soon as she begins working with our office.

When a birthmother is matched, whether she has been getting care or is beginning care, she may be willing to allow the adoptive mother to be a part of her doctor visits and attend ultrasounds. Many birthmothers will allow the adoptive parent(s) to be in the delivery room during the labor and birth. This is a great gift and, if they are comfortable doing so, we always suggest that our families accept this generous offer. It is an experience they will never forget.

Periodically, we receive calls from hospitals throughout the Los Angeles area when a woman has delivered a baby and wishes to place the baby for adoption. When this happens, we will talk with the birthmother and do some initial screening over the phone. If possible, we will go to the hospital with the necessary forms and letters from families who match the criteria she has given us during our initial conversation.

Occasionally, we are unable to go in person, and will have a more extensive phone conversation with birthmom to get her background, her health history and criteria for a family to adopt her baby. In both cases, we contact the family that she chooses, and the attorney and social worker, so that we can expedite the legal process necessary to move the adoption process forward within the hospital time frame.

Some birthmothers, who make a placement decision at the time of the birth of the baby, may have been considering this option during the pregnancy. However, in some cases, they have not received prenatal care. My sense is, this pregnancy may have been a stressful time and she may not have wished to take any action concerning it until it reached the point where the baby was here and some kind of action was necessary.

Many families have concern that if there has been no prenatal care, a birthmother may have a drug or alcohol problem, or some other issue that would prevent her from seeking medical care. This can make them wary of being open to a "hospital baby." While occasionally this can be the case, as it can with any situation, most often these are women who have life circumstances that make it impossible to bring a baby into their families at this time. These reasons can be many and varied.

A few years ago, a 15-year-old birthmother called us after delivering an 8 lb. baby boy. She claimed she didn't know she was pregnant. Laurie's parents were surprised when they took her to the hospital and discovered she was delivering a baby. The father of the baby was someone who worked in their employ, and I believe Laurie was fearful of the possibility that he would be fired, and that her parents would be disappointed in her once they discovered her pregnancy. For that reason, she hid it. Laurie was very healthy and had not abused any substances. She was just very young and fearful.

As it turned out, her parents were loving and supportive and understood her situation. The employee was reported and fired because their daughter was underage. Laurie and her mother decided on adoption for the baby, and they chose John and Carrie to parent her baby son. They shared the same faith and Laurie felt a connection with their letter. As it happened, John and Carrie had adopted their first daughter from the same hospital 4 years earlier.

Recently, we had a young birthmother who had a 4-year-old daughter and gave birth to a baby girl. She contacted me through the Social Services Dept. of the hospital and I met with her. She was lovely and chose a family with another child. She and the baby were both very healthy with no drug or alcohol history. She had not had prenatal care. She was living with her sister and had just been laid off by a supermarket where she had worked for 2 years. She knew she could not take care of another child, and wanted the best for her baby. This young woman was centered and very sweet and this case was one of the most pleasant and joyful we have had.

Drug And/Or Alcohol Use During The Pregnancy

Obviously, this is a sensitive area for birthmothers and for adoptive parents alike. We are committed, during this phase of the screening; to make the birthmother aware we have no judgment on what she has done. The truth is, there is a family for the baby, no matter what the situation, but we need to know the full reality of the circumstances. The family will, then, be equipped with the information necessary to be able to meet baby's needs. Since this is a difficult thing to discuss, some birthmothers will hold back some information. They may admit to using drugs, but may not want to tell us how regularly they are using, and how much.

One birthmother told me she had used cocaine 3 times. I have difficulty believing that cocaine use is easily limited to 3 times. I usually tell my families that if a birthmother tells us she has used drugs during her pregnancy, it is possible or even probable it is an ongoing issue. In that case, we feel it is advantageous to find a family who is prepared to take on any issues that might surface from drug use during the pregnancy. When we find those families, we have seen miracles occur and it is clear these babies are exactly where they are supposed to be. Their families were aware of their birth history and have been able and committed to meeting every need that may arise.

On the other side of that, a drug history does not necessarily come with a sentence of some kind of disability or serious issue. One of our birthmothers gave birth to a set of twins. Even though we were screening her weekly, she still managed to use between screenings. The twins were born about a month early, weighing about 4 pounds each. They are 15 now, are doing extremely well in school, and have no problems that seem to have come from the drug use. The odds may be against this kind of result, but we have seen cases where the babies are not seriously affected.

We believe much of this is connected to the kind, frequency of use, and longevity of use. All of this should be taken into consideration, and a decision made based on the circumstances and commitment.

If your family is not prepared to parent a drug-exposed baby, this is not a reason to feel guilty. If this is not comfortable for your family, it is best not to go forward should that scenario be presented as a possibility. There are families willing and waiting for babies with these issues. It takes courage to admit this is not for your family. You will find your little one, and the baby that goes to another family as a result of being drug exposed during pregnancy, will go to the family that is ready and prepared for whatever comes.

Other Health Issues With The Baby

This is also the case with a baby who is born with a health problem that was unknown during the pregnancy. We had a case with a birthmother who was healthy and receiving care during her pregnancy. She worked with a single adopting mother who had an 8-year-old son. The adoptive mother was a professional woman whose job allowed some flexibility. She and her son were anxious to adopt a baby and add to their family. Kim and Maryann met and formed an instant connection. They went through the last weeks of the pregnancy together, both looking forward to the birth of Kim's baby girl. After the birth, there were signs that all was not right with the baby. After a series of tests, it was discovered the baby had Down Syndrome.

Maryann called me and told me the situation. I told her I would be right there. She said, "No. I'm fine and I will stay here with Kim and the baby. Would you please look into finding a family for her? I need to know they will both be okay before I can leave them."

Maryann was single with a child. She worked and felt she could not give the baby everything she would need, and be fair to her son; since she had no partner or outside help. She told me she wanted the best for the baby and for her son, and, although it was breaking her heart, believed it would be best to find another family for the baby.

She and Kim had discussed it, and Kim understood and was open to meeting a family that was equipped to meet this baby's specific needs.

I called a family who had contacted our office about a month earlier. They were interested in adopting a baby with special needs. The adoptive mom had been caring for a 2-year-old who had Down Syndrome. The entire family was prepared and ready to adopt this beautiful baby. And, as it turned out, they lived 5 minutes from the hospital where Kim and the baby were waiting. We all believed this was meant to be. They took their baby home the next day, and we stayed in touch with Kim. She and the family have ongoing contact and a strong relationship. Maryann went on to adopt a daughter about 6 months later.

My theory is, and I've had lots of experience to back it up, these babies always go where they will have their individual needs met. And, I believe adoptive families always get the babies that are theirs. We know this with our own children. I am a firm believer that you get the one you're supposed to get and you'll know it when it happens.

Who Is She?

I am often asked "What kind of girl or woman is willing to place her baby for adoption?"

There is no unique personality type of birthmother. Each birthmother's story is as personal as our own stories are to us. Our job, as we screen women who wish to place their babies, is to listen to and hear each individual situation and what brought this girl/woman to us for assistance in forming an adoption plan for her baby.

Our job is to talk with her and listen carefully to the situations in her life that brought her to this decision. With girls who are very young, (13 to 17), although they can legally place their babies with or without parental consent, we want to spend extra time. It's important to be sure she truly understands adoption is forever. There is a fixed period of time she can reclaim the baby, usually 3 or 4 days, to 30 days;

dependent on whether the adoptive family is working with an agency or a private attorney. That is the law in California. Each state has its' own legal requirements. Please check with your legal representatives to get certainty about the laws where you reside. Once the legal time period has passed, her rights will be irrevocably terminated and she cannot take the baby back. The law may state she is declared an emancipated minor. However, the majority of young birthmothers, whether they are aware or whether they admit it, need the support of family during this time. Their care and concern can help them with the transition from being pregnant to delivering and placing a baby. They are unaware of the scope of emotions that will be present throughout that time.

She may wish to place her baby for all the right reasons. She may understand she's too young to parent and has no way to care for or finance raising a child. However, she will experience intense feelings when it's time to let go.

No matter how much preparation we give her or she receives from other birthmothers or adoption professionals, she will need support to allow her to proceed when it's time to say goodbye to her baby. She will be told that counseling from a licensed professional is available and she'll be urged to avail herself of the help. Some do and some don't; but we let her know the benefits of counseling can really help her.

With young girls, we are always grateful when there is family support for the adoption plan, especially from her mother. A supportive mom can make all the difference between success and failure. We've had successful placements with and without parental agreement and support, but it is always helpful to have mom involved.

With any birthmother, regardless of her age, the decision to place a baby comes with a lot of soul searching and deep feelings. Most of the women with whom we've worked over the years, have struggled long and hard to come to this decision.

We've had birthmothers from the ages of 14 through 41 and every age between. Each one has her own personal story. Although it's impossible to put ourselves in her shoes, our job is to assist her in being clear about her decision to place or not place her baby. If she opts to place, our job is to listen to her requirements for a family for her baby and show her profiles of families whose values and lifestyles reflect her wishes.

Whoever she is and whatever her age, it's the job of all of us involved, professionally and personally, to understand the level of sacrifice she is experiencing. We want to be sure she is informed about every phase of the process and about the family who will adopt her baby. All of this will bring her more peace.

What Is She Looking For In A Family For Her Baby?

Most birthmothers have an idea of what qualities, interests, and belief systems are important to them in choosing a family for their babies. We feel it's a meaningful part of our job to discuss this before we begin to present families.

We ask them if religion is a factor, or their ages, if other biological or adopted children are okay? Also, do they want someone local or is a family out of town or out of state comfortable for them? We also ask if there are any other desires or considerations concerning the family.

Most birthmothers tell us they just want a family that will love and provide a happy and productive life for their babies.

If that's the case, we work to find families that will resonate with her, emotionally. The birthmother's peaceful mind is critically important. If she knows the family and feels in her heart they will love and cherish her child and provide the life she wants for the baby, the adoption has a much better likelihood of succeeding.

If the match is made a period of time prior to the birth of the baby, it will give the adoptive mother and birthmother a chance to bond and build a level of trust between them that is invaluable.

If the baby has already been born, there is less time for that to occur, but valuable time at the hospital before release of birthmother and of baby will be helpful to all.

The screening process is the beginning of the relationship with the birthmother. The purpose is to get clear on her life, circumstances, and clarity and level of commitment regarding the adoption process. It also provides information on the father of the baby, her health and immediate issues that will give us an idea of how to proceed. It's a critical process. Of

7.

The Match

How Does The Match Happen?

In our office, we will work with you to determine the criteria that are important to you regarding your birthmother and baby. We then begin to search for a birthmother whose wishes for a family to adopt her baby match yours for a birthmother.

When we get a call from a birthmother interested in placing, during the screening, we determine what kind of family she believes is right for her baby. We then choose 4-7 profiles of families we feel will be open to her needs and situation, and the reverse. We call the families we have pulled and describe her health, financial and emotional needs. Before we present families, we want to be sure they understand this birthmother's individual situation. This enables us to get a picture of whether they feel they will be comfortable taking the next step, should she choose them.

We either send or bring those profiles to the birthmother, and arrange to talk with her after she has had an opportunity to review them. We ask her to choose a first choice and one backup, if, for some reason the first choice doesn't feel right to either or both parties.

While it is important to be as specific as you feel you need to be, it is wise to remember that the right baby may not be coming in the exact package you have pictured. If you feel you can be somewhat flexible, it might be a good idea to let your adoption professional know your strong preferences. Let them know you can be called if you are open to a situation that may not fit all your criteria.

A few years ago we worked with a family that was very clear they were only open to being presented to a birthmother who had certainty the baby was carrying was a girl. That was their only criteria. About three months later, we received a call from a young woman who had had an ultrasound that confirmed she was carrying a girl. She chose their letter. They talked and met and everyone was very happy with the match.

Birthmother Elizabeth, and adoptive mom Sheri, spent many hours together prior to the birth of the baby. When the baby was born, adoptive mom, Sheri called us to let us know Elizabeth had delivered a baby boy. We were all surprised and concerned this might affect Sheri's and her husband Tom's decision to move forward with their adoption plan. Before I could ask her how she was feeling about it, she said, "Oh, Nikki, he's so beautiful! I can't imagine why I ever thought we wanted a girl. He is definitely our son!" She hasn't stopped bragging about him since!

If you get a call about a specific birthmother, it's pretty certain you will be excited. Try to listen carefully, about the specifics before agreeing to talk with her. This way, if she chooses you, you will be armed with the right information. That should preclude any significant surprises that could cause upset during your conversation. We will gather as much information as possible about financial and health issues, and screen as thoroughly as we can in all other pertinent areas. Of course, as we go forward through the remainder of the pregnancy, more information will come forward. During the match, we should have a pretty good idea of the important issues; at least enough that we can determine who may be comfortable with this particular situation. If, after you speak with the birthmother you have a specific worry, be sure to clear it, as much as is possible, with your adoption professional.

If you choose to take the next step and meet with her, or, if she is out-of-state, to talk and move forward, it is important to have resolved any problem areas that might have been of concern. That way, at the meeting if all goes well, you will all be ready and on the same page to form an adoption plan.

While it is extremely painful for adoptive parents when they are not chosen by a birthmother, it is very difficult for birthmothers, when they have selected a family and the family decides not to go forward. Birthmothers often take that very personally; not just a rejection of them, but also of their babies. Sometimes, birthmothers take this as a sign that they are supposed to keep their babies, although they know they are not in a position to do so. The baby may be going into a situation that she wanted to avoid. Therefore, we are as careful as we can be that before any match, any potential problem that has been disclosed has been addressed.

The good news is, in my experience of over 20 years working in adoption, I have only seen one of the parties decide not to move forward with a match, a handful of times. Almost always, it is love at first sight and the matches move forward smoothly.

How Long Before The Baby Is Born Do We Match?

The match can occur anytime between around 6 months of pregnancy up to and after the birth of the baby. Some birthmothers come to us around the end of their second trimester. We feel comfortable beginning to work with them at this time because they have usually had a month or month-and-a-half to have begun to feel the baby move. There has also been some time to be aware of the reality of the pregnancy. At that point they are usually ready to consider the possibility of adoption as an option, if circumstances warrant it.

We also work with birthmothers who have delivered their babies and want to place at the hospital, and at any point in between.

Dependent upon when the birthmother comes to us and wishes to be matched with a family, there are strong advantages to having whatever time you have to get to know her. This woman is the person who will bring your dream of family to reality. She is allowing you to raise her precious baby. It's important to know her gifts, her abilities, her likes and dislikes, as well as her life story if she is willing to share it. And, of course, you will want to have as much medical history as is available on both birthparents.

One of our birthmothers, Sarah, came to our office when she was 38 weeks pregnant. We went through the paperwork and medical history, birthfather situation, etc., and when it was time to discuss what she was looking for in a family for her baby, she was not specific. I showed her 4 families who might be a good match and she immediately chose Chuck and Joyce. Since she was so close to giving birth, she was concerned she might not have time to give them the family background information she wanted them to have.

They met for dinner the following night and, the next day Sarah went into labor. Joyce was with Sarah throughout her labor and delivery, and the hospital was able to provide a room for Joyce and Chuck during Sarah's and the baby's hospital stay. Joyce has told us many times, how valuable that time with Sarah was for her and Chuck. They learned a lot about her history and background, and her skills and abilities. Now they have very valuable information to share with their daughter.

When our son, Charlie, was born, we had an opportunity to have a few visits with his birthmother prior to his birth, and learned about the athletic abilities both she and the birthfather shared. She was a dance teacher and he a skilled football player.

Charlie developed his skill and love of figure skating, starting at about 4 years, and over the next 9 years. It has been good for him to know about his birth history.

If you have a preference about how long you are comfortable waiting to be matched, be sure to relate this to your adoption professional. If you do this, be aware that every condition you place on your adoption plan can add time to your wait. Of course, no professional can give you a definite time frame, but the more flexible you can be, usually, the faster you will match. That doesn't mean you shouldn't be as specific as you need to be, but do think about what is truly most important to you. If there is a requirement you feel you may be able to relax some, it may shorten your wait to do so.

Waiting for the match is a very difficult proposition. You may feel helpless and frustrated. We usually tell our clients this is the most difficult part. Although that's the part that is handled by the professionals, it's a good idea to keep a few birthmother presentation profiles or letters in your car. Spread the word, everywhere you go, you are looking to adopt a baby. The hairdresser or the person at the dry cleaners, or at your place of worship or work, may know someone who knows someone who is pregnant. Should that ever be the case, you can give them a copy of your letter and alert your adoption professionals. If there is interest on both sides, he or she can do the screening and facilitate the match.

Will Someone Be With Us When We Meet Her?

Different offices have different policies about this issue. Many offices feel it is important to have a representative present when the potential family and the birthmother meet. They believe someone should monitor and guide the conversation so that they will cover all the major issues and any red flags on either side can be addressed there.

Other offices, ours included, feel the initial meeting is best between the family and the birthmother/birthparents. If there is a third party there, the participants will likely look to the third person to move the conversation along. This will inhibit any natural dialogue between them. We tell our families and our birthparents that there are no off-limit topics, and they should feel free to ask questions. The one direction we are very clear to provide our adoptive families is not to "interrogate" the birthmother. Often, there are issues that are important to the adoptive family, about which they may be worried or anxious. We let them know, should these things be really important to them, they should feel free to address them; but to watch their level of intensity when doing so. When we screen our birthmothers, there are certain "hot button" issues about which many adoptive parents have concerns.

These issues might include drug or alcohol use, or financial needs, contact after birth, etc. We want to cover those so when we present families, we are as certain as possible that all are on the same page or those issues will not impede a potential match. We try to be as certain as we can be that there won't be any unpleasant discoveries or surprises during the match process. If all decide to match, the attorneys and agencies get involved and will deal with these concerns in depth. This meeting is solely for the purpose of spending time getting to know each other. The relationship between birthmother and adoptive family is a critical one. Everything else can and should be handled once that is confirmed.

We suggest the family take the birthmother to lunch or dinner somewhere close to her home. They will often ask if they can bring her flowers or a small gift. This is another area where you must check with your attorney about the laws in your state regarding gifts to birthmothers. In California, this is legal and we believe it is a nice gesture.

We ask that all participants call us after the meeting to tell us how it went. Most of the time, we hear from both adoptive and birthparents how much they have discovered they have in common. They will usually have common interests that may include a love of animals, theatre, movies, cultural events, cooking, gardening, and so on. Many birthmothers would love to know their babies will have the opportunity to travel. If that is a part of your life, be sure to add the information in your letter and talk about it when you meet. Talk about your work and family. Birthmothers are usually anxious to know there is an extended family waiting to love the baby. Those kinds of interests, hobbies and family, will begin a bond that will help throughout the process and beyond.

It is usually this meeting that cements the match. Once that has happened, we encourage families and birthmothers to stay in contact regularly throughout the remainder of the pregnancy. It's good to discuss the upcoming birth and work with the attorney or agency to formulate a plan. Talk with her about how much and what kind of contact she would like to have with you before and during the birth. Some birthmoms will want the adoptive family, most particularly the adoptive mother, to be with her at doctor appointments, during labor, etc. Some are not comfortable with this. It's another thing to know and for which to be prepared.

With respect to after birth contact, most professionals will get as clear a picture as is possible from both adoptive and birth parents as to what their wishes and preferences are regarding this issue prior to getting them in contact with each other. Does birthmom want photos and letters? Does she want visitation, and, if so, how much? Does she want no contact at all? This is an essential area where agreement about what is wanted is critical; so we want to be sure all are on the same page about after birth contact before the match.

When you have matched, it is time to get the legal representatives involved. Whether you're with an agency or planning an independent adoption with an attorney, the legal process begins with the match. At that point, the hospital will be notified of the adoption plan and given identifying information about the birthmother and the prospective adoptive family so they will be prepared for the birthmother's wishes during her hospital stay.

The match is important in all of this. If the birthmother is peaceful about her decision to place and her decision regarding a family for the baby, the entire process will go much smoother than if she is unfamiliar.

What Do We Talk About?

There are no off-limit topics during the meeting. Obviously, everyone involved will have questions that are of concern; and, of course they should be able to ask them. However, one thing we always stress to our potential families is that, of course, they will need to ask important questions. However, they must be aware of the attitude they are putting out there while asking. It's easy to fall into the trap of running question after question at her, without realizing you're doing it. She will have questions for you as well, and you want to give her as much opportunity as she needs to ask them, and answer them honestly and thoroughly.

Birthmother, Jerilyn, chose not to move forward with a possible family for her baby because they gave brief answers when she asked questions, and continuously followed their answers with several questions back at her, one after the other. She felt, as a result, they weren't really interested in a dialogue, or in her need to know more about them, and she was very uncomfortable. She felt that was not a good beginning for a relationship that is so important for all.

It's critical your birthmother knows you have an interest in her, as a person, not just as one birthmother described it, a baby machine. Birthmothers are very good at picking up signals from you.

When you go to meet her, expect to be nervous. The truth is, she is nervous, too. Some young women have told me their fear level is near panic because there is a risk you may not like her and may reject her. This decision to place her baby is so enormous and so personal for her, and she has already pushed through sadness and fears to an almost unbearable level just from that. Then, the next thing is to select a family. From her point of view, a rejection from a family, not just of her, but her baby as well, is almost too difficult. Most adoptive parents have no awareness of the level of risk and stress birthmothers feel around this most important meeting. They are going through their own terror of being rejected by her, or, worse yet, finding out something that may make this match impossible. They have been waiting, possibly for a year or more for this one meeting; as a result, are consumed with their own worry.

Since the adoptive parents are usually older, more experienced, and have more stability in their lives; we ask that they work to put aside their own fears, as much as possible. We ask that they try to have an awareness of and compassion for her concerns and just be with her. And, above all, try to have a good time. This is the beginning of a bond for life, whether there is an agreement for future contact or not. Enjoy your time with her and relax. You will look back on this meeting with fond memories as you raise your baby and see little mannerisms or looks that are reminiscent of his or her birthmother, and the beginning of your relationship with her.

What Happens Between The Match And The Birth Of The Baby?

Once the match has been agreed to by birthmother and adoptive family, the guidelines will be set for contact between the match and the birth.

Some families and birthmothers prefer a "closed" adoption and want no contact during the adoption process. This is not a common wish for families or for birthparents; but if that's a preference for either party, we work to find a match with someone whose criteria are the same.

If there is a period of weeks or months prior to the due date of the baby, and family and birthmother wish to be in contact with each other, an agreement will be set up so all are comfortable with whatever arrangements are made.

If your birthmother is local, and if you and she are both interested in contact, you will find during that time, you have common interests. It's likely that's what drew you to each other in the beginning. It's good to nurture those common likes. The time with your birthmother can give you both peace and an understanding of each other that's invaluable. When you talk or meet for the first time, you may want to discuss what kind of contact, and how often she would like. It's good to have a general idea of what works for both of you so your expectations and hers are in sync. This avoids any misunderstanding that can make for unnecessary upset on either end.

One of our families, Kevin and Joyce, were working with birthmother Marie, who was due about 9 weeks after the match. They formed an immediate bond, but all were concerned about what happened next. Family and birthmother wanted to get to know each other during the wait for the baby's arrival, but all were uncertain how to proceed.

They decided together, with some guidance from us and from their attorney, that phone contact a couple of times a week was appropriate, and they would get together at least every two weeks. Joyce spent some time with Marie at lunches; and on one visit, went shopping for maternity clothes. The time getting to know each other, waiting for the birth of the baby, allowed them all to feel more comfortable with each other during the birth and hospital stay.

If your birthmother is not local, and there is a physical distance between you that makes visits and outings together impossible, it's good to set up a phone schedule that works for you and for her. In this way, you can learn about each other and build enough of a relationship that you will be more comfortable when you arrive to meet your new baby. If there's a period of time prior to the due date of the baby, it might be a good thing to take a trip to her location for a day or two, just to see and meet her. This will give you an opportunity to get to know and learn about each other in a casual setting. This is also a time to meet her family and/or the birthfather of the baby; if the birthmother wants you to do so.

Many families have questions about how much contact they should have with their birthmothers. We generally suggest, if you're open, let her lead the way. It's okay to ask her how often she would like you to call or get together, and follow her guidelines. The benefit to both of you is the more contact you have, the more you will learn about each other, and the more information you will have about your child's history.

A birthmother, who is open to contact, will often allow you to share in the birth of the baby. Some adoptive parents are very excited about this possibility and some don't feel comfortable with the idea. Whatever you're feeling, know that its fine. It's a very personal decision and is completely up to you. We discuss this in the "Hospital" chapter of this book.

But, if you're comfortable being with the birthmother when she's in labor and delivering, from my own personal experience, I can say those moments are some of the most important in my life. To hold your birthmother's hand and be there when your baby enters the world is a great honor, and, for that moment, you are both the mothers of that baby.

I know it may feel scary to invest yourself in getting to know your birthmother. It feels very risky for several reasons. You may worry she could change her mind; and after you invest in getting to know and care about and for her, if that were to happen, it would be devastatingly painful. That makes sense, and it could happen; and if you feel that would be difficult to deal with, you're absolutely right. In sensitive areas and areas that can feel frightening or risky, it's essential to have professionals around who can support you through those times. You alone must decide which risks you are able or willing to take; but it's good to ask for support. If, in these cases, you are uncomfortable or unwilling, you must be true to what you feel.

However, it's a good idea, if your birthmother is open to sharing this most personal time with you, to weigh whether you can go forward on this part of the journey with her; knowing that whatever happens, you've had a valuable experience. If so, it's definitely worth the risk.

Enjoy your time with her. The truth is, this is the woman who is giving you your family, and anything you can learn about her will be beneficial to your child. Also, the more you know her, the more you will be able to share the memories and knowledge of who she is with genuine caring and respect.

What Happens When The Baby Has Been Born Before The Match?

Not infrequently, we may get a call from a local hospital telling us a woman has given birth and is requesting to place the baby for adoption. When that happens, we talk with the birthmother in order to find out her circumstances, her health history, her reasons for wanting to place, and whether there is any drug or alcohol history during the pregnancy. We also ask about any known mental health issues in either family. We want her to know there is a family for her baby and that whatever the issue, we can help her locate the right situation for her.

In some cases, she has had no prenatal care. There can be many reasons for that and we discuss with her why she didn't seek care for her pregnancy.

Most often, the assumption is she has been abusing some kind of substance. In every case and in every hospital where we have been associated, these women are tested, as a matter of course, for drugs, alcohol and AIDS. These screenings are done routinely; just as they would be when we meet a birthmother prior to the birth of the baby.

As we complete the screening process with a birthmother who has delivered and wants to place, we discuss what their preferences are in a family for the baby. Once we have completed this process, we will gather and call families who might have an interest in this situation. When we have found 3-6 families who are interested and ready to move immediately, we put together our questionnaire and some info about us, and the family letters, and head to the hospital.

There can be many reasons she has not received medical care prior to entering the hospital. In some cases, we've had young girls who didn't want their families to know they were pregnant. That sounds impossible, but I've seen it several times. Frequently, there may have been substance abuse, and the birthmother was fearful of the doctor discovering she was using. Of course, ultimately this will be discovered. She may, then, feel shame and embarrassment for having put the baby in this situation.

Aside from drug and alcohol exposure, there are rare occasions when a baby may be born with a medical condition that will require additional medical attention and care. When that happens, our goal is to find a family that is open to caring for a baby with potential health problems. There are families who are very open to adopting a special needs baby.

Veronica called us from a local hospital and said she had delivered a baby who may have Downs Syndrome. We contacted two families who had asked us to get in touch with them if a special needs baby should need a home. We contacted Megan and Tom and told them about this situation. They were delighted, and we discovered they were located within a half-hour of the hospital. I met with them at the hospital. They assured the doctors at the hospital and me they were ready to take on any issues that might come up for this baby. They also referred the doctors to their pediatrician and a resource for families of Down Syndrome babies, with whom they had met. This organization was on board and ready to help Megan and Tom in loving and caring for this baby.

Birthmother, Veronica met and loved them. They spent time with her in the hospital, and assured her they would provide all the love and care they would give any biological child; and how excited they were to move forward toward adopting this baby girl. Veronica spent time with the baby alone, to say goodbye. Megan and Tom and Veronica said goodbye and they took their baby daughter home.

Veronica cried after they left. I asked her what she was feeling. She said, "I am very sad I can't provide the care the baby will need. I miss her already and I feel guilty wondering if there was something I did wrong to create her Down Syndrome."

I hugged her and tried to reassure her, then called a social worker from the Patient Care Department and asked for someone to come and reassure her the baby's condition was not her fault. We then arranged for adoption counseling for her.

I spoke with Veronica a few weeks later. She said she was doing much better and was grateful for the counseling. "And," she said, "I'm so happy the baby is with Megan and Tom. I know they will give her every bit of love they have and will get her whatever professional help she needs. It's just been hard."

Megan and Tom report that baby Gina is doing great and surpassing every milestone.

There are families who are open to adopting a baby who has been drug-exposed. This is certainly not for everyone, but it's always a priority for us to find a placement in order to keep these babies from going into the system. The majority of families are not comfortable adopting a baby with possible drug or alcohol exposure. Others may have judgment on that decision. However, this is a deeply personal decision for each family.

8.

Getting Ready For Baby

Should We Start Buying Things? What About A Shower?

The answers to these questions are completely dependent on what you feel works best for you and your family. Some families are uncomfortable purchasing anything ahead of the birth of the baby. They may choose to have a bag with diapers, a sleeper, a blanket, and anything else basic they feel they will need if they get a call with an immediate situation.

They may have an idea for the theme of the baby's room or names for the baby. However, they may choose to wait until there is a baby before they move forward with any of the preparations. Some choose not to tell family or friends they have been pursuing adoption or are matched. This is an individual decision. None of us knows what's best for a waiting family.

When adoptive families ask me about my thoughts on whether to purchase baby items or furniture in advance, I suggest they look at what feels right to them. By the time a family gets into the adoption process, usually they are ready for a baby yesterday. Some are fearful to let themselves get excited about baby shopping, names, etc. They may have been through stress and disappointment over failed infertility treatments, or have had to witness friends and family celebrating births, showers, etc. and are gun shy.

If this is the case, I suggest they begin to think about names, and possibly, go to the baby department of their local department stores. Walk through, and maybe buy a t-shirt or a blanket. Start off with something small. It may be helpful to allow themselves to feel the joy that someone is on the way for them and it will be real.

After years of wanting this so much, it's difficult to open your heart(s) and believe it can happen. If that's the case, I usually suggest taking these small steps may be a way to move into accepting the possibility that it will happen for you.

As with every part of this process each, family must go forward based on their own instincts; but please consider that this doesn't only happen for everyone else. It will happen for you, too.

Some families may wish to have everything in place prior to the birth or even as soon as they begin the process. When we adopted our first, we did purchase a crib and bedding, some baby clothing and bottles. We felt it was an affirmation that our baby was coming. It was just a feeling we had and we wanted, very much, to get ready.

When we met our son Jimmy's birthmother, we were beside ourselves excited. We told our families about the match. They asked if it was all right if they planned a shower for us. We thought about it and decided it would be wonderful to have the people closest to us come together and share our joy.

Two days before the shower, our birthmother disappeared. She had moved and we were unable to locate her. We were devastated. We thought about canceling the shower, but decided to go forward with it. We knew our baby would come to us; whether or not it was this one. We still felt hope that this birthmother would come back, but knew we couldn't get invested in waiting for that to happen. And, we knew in our hearts, we must move forward knowing we wanted this baby, but without attachment. Not easy! But it was the only solution. We felt the shower might help us remember the original goal, parenting.

The shower was on a Sunday. It was a wonderful event and everyone there gave us encouragement and shared our belief we would find the right baby. That was an enormous help and big confirmation for us.

Two days later we, received a call from our attorney. "Nikki, I heard from Maggie. She found new housing through her worker at Salvation Army, and is living in your area. She asked me to get in touch with you and Michael to ask if you'd like to continue working with her.

She asked if you could meet her at the same place you met initially. If you're up for that, she'll be there at 4:30 today."

It took about 15 seconds to mumble, "We'll be there."

Our meeting went very well. We continued on with Maggie, and two weeks later our beautiful boy entered the world. I was in the delivery room and got to witness his birth. Michael was outside the room waiting to meet his son. Friends and family were in the waiting room. In our case, sharing every part of the time surrounding the birth of our son was a positive experience.

In another case, Steve and Penny chose to keep their relationship with their birthmother, Joanna, between only them, us, and their attorney. Penny was excited to go to doctor appointments with Joanna and loved their relationship. It was difficult for them to keep it from their parents and friends, but they felt it was best for all concerned. They knew the people who cared for them would have a very difficult time if the adoption didn't go forward. When Joanna delivered their daughter, Monica, they were able to call everyone from the hospital, and when they got home with the baby, there was a huge welcoming committee waiting for them.

There are no rules to any of this. Every decision is deeply personal to every family, and it's important to understand and honor whatever choice is right for you.

When Do We Tell Our Other Children And Family Members We're Going to Adopt?

Our belief is, if you choose to talk with your children about adopting a baby, it's good to do so, initially, in general terms. For little children, you might begin to talk about having a new baby brother or sister. Little ones, especially under 5, don't need a lot of detail.

And, with children of any age, we feel the goal is to protect them from the disappointment and upset that would occur if there's a problem anywhere throughout the process. While it's exciting to know there will be a new sibling, it's difficult for them to understand the waiting.

There are some wonderful books that can guide families on how and when to talk to their children about adoption. Check online or at your local book stores or library for topics that are appropriate for your family.

Older children may enjoy participating in the preparations for a new baby. Nate and Karen have a son who was 8 when they began their second adoption journey. They felt he was old enough to be part of the process. Jordan had been asking for a baby brother or sister. When Nate and Karen told him they would be adopting a baby, he wanted to draw a picture of himself, mommy and daddy, and his new brother or sister. They used his drawing for the back page of their birthmother letter. Each birthmother to whom we showed their letter loved his drawing.

A few months later, Nate and Karen were matched with birthmother Janelle. They felt very comfortable with her. However, they felt it important to keep Jordan separate from any involvement until after the baby was born. They waited until Janelle had signed the paperwork to release the baby into their care to take home from the hospital. Right before the baby was released, Karen brought Jordan to the hospital to meet his new brother and Janelle.

Only you know your children, and your immediate and extended family. Make a decision on how much information you are ready to share and when to share it. However, take into consideration whether there will be constant questions from well-meaning friends and family members that may cause you additional stress. They may want to be kept informed at every step.

They may feel it their responsibility to question every decision you make, and/or the sincerity of the birthmother. These may be well-meaning, and are likely meant to help and support, but can create a responsibility on your part to explain or defend.

This time is anxiety producing, even under the best of circumstances. It's a time to nurture and to preserve your energy in whatever way works best for you.

Our dearest friend, Nan, asked us, a week before the birth of our son, what we had to be stressed about. We had no idea how to begin to explain our concerns to her, or our anticipation about becoming parents of a new baby.

There's a lot to focus on at this time. Take care of yourselves and allow the joy in as well. During the match, prior to the birth of your baby, it's a good idea to create as stress-free an environment as possible so that you can be fully present for your baby and your birthmother.

9.

The Hospital

The hospital experience is terrifying, exciting and stressful; frequently all at the same time. This is the time you and the birthmother will share the birth of your baby; something for which you have waited for a long while. It is also the time the birthmother is at her most vulnerable; and, for you, the threat of losing your precious baby seems more real than at any other. Birthmothers that come to us prior to the birth of their babies are asked to form a plan; letting us know their preferences during the hospital experience.

What Are The Birthmother's Rights?

The hospital is the birthmother's territory. She will be asked her wishes in many areas about and during her stay there. It will be her choice who will be with her during her labor and the delivery of the baby. If she is willing to allow the adoptive parents (usually just the adoptive mother) to be with her at that time, and you are comfortable doing so, I can say from personal experience, this is a wonderful gift. There is nothing more exciting and miraculous than watching and participating in the birth of your baby. Some adoptive parents are a bit uncomfortable sharing that experience with the birthmother and that's perfectly fine. You alone know what works for you. But, it's definitely something to think about and a great privilege should she offer the option. The moment of the baby's birth is also an amazing bonding experience for you and the birthmother. For that moment, you are both involved in bringing this precious baby into the world and, whether or not you have an agreement for contact after the birth, this will be an experience you will likely cherish forever.

She'll also be asked whether she wants to see, feed, and hold the baby, or if she wants the adoptive family to take care of him, or if she wants all of them to do it together.

A small number of birthmothers wish to care for their babies, exclusively. This can be a red flag and is very stressful for the family. This is not common and, in my experience, does not mean it's a given the birthmother will keep the baby. Most birthmothers choose to share care of the baby during their stay in the hospital. Some do not. If she wishes to be moved out of the maternity area after the birth, most hospitals will move her to another floor so she'll be out of earshot of babies crying and the activities involved around the babies there. I'm always a bit sad when this is the case, because she is not allowing herself the opportunity to see and say goodbye to her baby. However, this is a deeply personal decision, and I've learned over the years, to respect whatever choice each birthmother makes.

A few years ago, one of our birthmothers decided she wanted to care, exclusively, for the baby during the hospital stay. This was unusual and very stressful for the adoptive family. Ken and Judy were at the hospital throughout the baby's stay. Edith, the birthmother, kept the baby in her room except for a few brief periods when she allowed the baby to be taken to the nursery so the family could see and hold him. All of us had concern about how Edith would handle leaving the hospital without the baby and whether she'd really be able to say goodbye to him. At the end of her stay, she called Ken and Judy into her room, handed them the baby, allowed them to dress him, held him for a minute, kissed him and said goodbye to all of them, and left the hospital. She made the commitment to the adoption and followed through. The baby, Mark, is now 8 years old, and his adoptive family is still in contact with Edith through photos and letters.

Edith has moved on, gone to college, and is currently working as a nurse. Mark is thriving and is a happy, healthy boy; and his family says, now, they wouldn't have had it any other way.

Another birthmother, Kelly, opted to move to another floor in the hospital and wanted no contact with the baby or the family. The adoptive family Kelly had chosen was from out-of-state, and wanted, very much, to meet and thank her for allowing them to adopt and parent their beautiful boy. Kelly was firm she did not want to meet them. At the end of her stay, I approached her once more and told her of their desire to let her know, personally, how much adopting this baby meant to them and their family. She said,

"When I leave, I'd be grateful if you could take me past the nursery so I can see them with the baby."

On her way out, I wheeled her by the nursery window. Marcia was feeding the baby and looking at him tenderly. Bob was sitting next to her, holding the baby's hand. He had a tear running down his cheek. Kelly smiled and said, "I can go now." I took her to the car and a friend drove her home. Bob and Marcia send me a photo of their son, John, every year. I've saved them all and they'll be here if Kelly wants them.

As I said earlier, the most common situation in our experience is that the birthmother will want to share the care of the baby with the family. This can be wonderful for the birthmother and for the family. Having the family involved in the baby's care gives the birthmother a chance to see how much love the family feels for this new little life and the care and concern that goes into each interaction. It also gives the birthmother and adoptive mother a chance to get to learn more about each other. In some cases, the birthmother will want the baby to be moved to the nursery at night so she can rest. In that case, some hospitals, if they have room, will allow the family to stay in a separate room with the baby.

During her hospital stay, the birthmother will be asked to fill out a birth certificate. Again, please check with your attorney or agency regarding the laws in your state regarding all phases of your adoption. In California, the birthmother may choose a name for the baby.

Some birthmothers have been thinking of a name about which they feel strongly. She may give the baby whichever name she chooses. Or, if she has no wish to name the baby, she can choose to use the first and middle name you have chosen, or simply put baby girl or boy on the certificate. That document will be called the "working" birth certificate and will be on the record until the adoption is finalized. A few months later, you will receive an "amended" birth certificate with your name(s) as parent(s) and the name you have given the baby. That will be the birth certificate used by the child throughout his life.

The birthmother will also be asked what her preferences are when it's time to leave the hospital. Does she want to bring an outfit and dress the baby or does she want the family to do it? She'll make the choice about whether she wants to leave the hospital first, or if she wants you to take the baby first, or if she wants you all to leave together. If she needs a ride home, be sure one of you can take her. The only option offered to the family by the hospital staff is, if the baby is a boy, whether or not they want a circumcision done there. The family will make this decision because it impacts their family and not the birthmother's.

Who Will Be With Her When She Delivers The Baby?

Does she want you to be there during labor and delivery? If so, in what capacity? Does she want you to be her labor coach? Does she want you to just be with her? Does she want you to wait in the waiting room? Many birthmothers want to share the entire experience with you. Some may want their mothers or other family members to be there. Some may want the birthfather to share this time with them. We will discuss her options and ask her how she wants it to be for her. At that point a letter, either from us or from the attorney, will be sent to the hospital, advising them of her wishes.

They can make notes to accommodate her preferences when she arrives. Of course we know plans can change, but at the time we discuss them with her, we will have a tentative plan.

If I/We Are Allowed In The Delivery Room, Who Will Hold The Baby After He/She Is Born?

The birthmother will be asked if she wants the baby placed in her arms or if she wants you to hold her first. She may wish to see and hold the baby first, and hand her to you. Or, she may want the baby given directly to you. Her peace of mind, especially during this time, is very important. She needs to feel you are there with her to support her, not to snatch the baby and run. At some times during this process, that will probably be your deepest desire. This is the time to count on the trust you have built with your birthmother, and to remember how difficult this is for her. Now is the time to call out your compassion as you never have before.

How Much Time Will We Spend With The Baby? How Much Time Will We Spend With The Birthmother?

All of this is up to the birthmother. Some birthmothers want the adoptive family to fully care for the baby during the hospital stay. Some birthmothers will want to care for their babies on their own, or with family, during the stay. Many, if not most, will want to share the time with the adoptive family and the baby. They may, especially, want the adoptive mother, to be there. It's important for some birthmothers to have the opportunity to see the adoptive family's interaction with the baby. If this is the birthmother's choice, it's a wonderful time to learn more about her and further strengthen your bond. In this case, if you are able, and if she wishes you to do so, it's a good idea to spend the night with her in her room.

If not, we advise our birthmothers to see if their moms, baby's birthfather, or someone else can stay with them overnight. We have had cases where hospital personnel, mostly nurses, have come into the room in the night, when they are sleeping and vulnerable, and attempted to convince them to keep their babies.

Our birthmother, Marie, who was 30 at the time of the birth of her baby, reported three nurses entered her room and said, "What? Are you a dog, you give your children away?"

Another told us at around midnight a nurse came in and said, "You might as well throw your baby in the trash if you're going to let someone else have it!"

This is devastating, and will, most likely, not happen if someone is with her.

Marie told me, "I'm 30 years old, and an adult. I was able to tell them to go. But, I was wondering what could have happened if I was a 15-year-old girl and alone? This would have been 3 adults pushing her."

We always let our birthmothers know, and inform each of them, that if someone approaches her in this way, she should get their names and ask them to leave. We will then report it to the appropriate hospital authorities.

Should We Give Her A Gift?

If your state allows it, absolutely!! We recommend you write a card telling her how grateful you are and what parenting this baby means to you. And, depending on whether or not she wants contact after the birth, give her an appropriate gift. If your agreement with her is to send letters and photos periodically, or, possibly, visitation, a good gift might be a silver locket where she can keep a picture of the baby. A nice photo frame is also a good possibility.

If she doesn't want contact after she leaves the hospital, it might be nice to get her an outfit to wear home, or a basket from Crabtree and Evelyn, or Bath and Body Works. This is generally, something she would not or may be unable to buy for herself.

What Do We Do If She Wants Time Alone With The Baby?

This will probably be difficult for you, but may be one of the most important moments for your birthmother. She may need to have time to talk with the baby alone, hold, kiss, and say goodbye. It's important for the birthmother to have that opportunity. However, it's not easy for the family.

I usually advise my families, when she expresses the need for time with the baby, to give her a hug and leave the room. If you are fearful or distressed, it's a good idea to call your adoption professionals and allow them to provide support for you.

How Long Will She Be There?

If she gives birth naturally, the hospital stay is usually 1-2 days. In the event of a C-section, it is usually 2-4 days. If she has other children and you are matched in advance of the birth, it's important to see that arrangements have been made for their care during her hospital stay. You will want to assist her in making a plan for them. Knowing they are cared for will make her stay more peaceful, and you will be able to focus on her and the baby. She may have family or a friend that will care for them. Dependent on the laws in your state, you will need to check with your agency or adoption attorney to see if you are allowed to provide payment for these services. If possible, that should be in place prior to the birth of the baby. You will also want to be sure she has transportation to and from the hospital. If she needs a ride home, you will want to be available for that. Also, be sure she has groceries and any medication she needs. Again, check with your adoption professionals regarding any possible liability.

When Can We Take The Baby Home?

In California, the answer to this will be dependent on two things. First, the pediatrician will need to clear the baby for release. This usually happens 24-48 hours after birth, if there are no complications. The other consideration is the birthmother. We usually suggest following her lead in this decision. Some birthmothers want their babies to leave after they leave the hospital. Some are okay if the baby leaves ahead. Some want all to leave together.

She will be asked if she wants to dress the baby. She may have an outfit for you to take him home, or she may want you to bring an outfit and dress him. If she needs a ride home, it may be a good idea to get her released and taken home and then come back for the baby.

Again, each states has its' own laws about all phases of the adoption process. Talk with your agency or attorney to be clear how this part of the process works for you.

What Has To Happen For The Legal Process At The Hospital?

Since this varies from state to state, be sure you have an understanding of what is required in your state. Work with your agency and/or adoption attorney in advance, in order to form a plan. When your birthmother goes into labor, you can contact your attorney and/or agency so they will be aware and available to you during the hospital stay; as when they are involved, they will be able to ensure everything is handled in an efficient manner.

What Happens If Something Is Wrong With The Baby?

While this is always a possibility, it is not, by any means, a common occurrence. This is rare, but it is important to think about what you would be prepared to handle. And, you also must take a long look at what you are not equipped or comfortable taking on. If you don't believe you can go forward with the adoption of a baby with special needs, and that turns out to be the case, please don't feel you are abandoning the baby if you don't feel you can move forward. There will be a family for that baby, and it will be the right one. It's not fair to you or, especially to the baby to take on a situation that would be a burden to you. Resentment would build and this baby needs your unconditional love and support. There are people who are looking for special needs babies. They are fully capable and are waiting with open arms for an opportunity to parent such a baby.

There is one piece of advice I like to give my families about the hospital. That is, remember your birthmother will, most likely, have no idea this experience is stressful for you. She is focused on giving birth and saying goodbye to her baby. In her mind, you're going home with a baby, and she's going home with nothing. What do you have to be upset about?

This is normal, very appropriate, and accurate. We know and understand your stress and fear levels are extreme at this time. Being in love with your baby and still having to wait 1-2 days to go home and begin your life as a family is extremely difficult. You are there with the woman who gave birth to the child for whom you have been waiting, for a very long time. You are already in love with the baby and wonder how she can possibly let go.

This is a good time to allow family and friends to support you. Your adoption professionals will also be available to help keep you grounded and balanced until you take your precious little one home.

Despite the stress and fear, try not to lose the experience of the hospital time with your birthmother and baby. There is much to treasure and remember about those days. Later, you will want to share this with your child as a wonderful time of being a part of his coming into the world. You'll get through it, and, as your baby grows, you'll look back on this time fondly.

10.

After We Come Home

The best advice we can give is to make the time right after your return home as peaceful as possible. This is a time to get to know your baby and focus on becoming a family. If you have other children, let them take time to meet the baby and be a part of this most important time. If close family members want to visit, and it's likely they will, enjoy that time. However, it might be good to limit the time and numbers of visitors during the first few days.

You'll be figuring out a schedule that's comfortable for you and your baby and children. Sleep as much as you can, so that you'll have the energy to provide for the time and needs your new baby will require.

Once you get acquainted and somewhat organized, it's a wonderful time to show off your new addition to the people who mean the most to you. Take in the "oohs and ahhs and the comments about how beautiful your baby is. This is such a special time for all of you. Congratulations! Treasure this journey. It's worth every minute!!!

Post-Birth Contact With Birthparents

During the match with your birthmother, you have probably made some post-birth agreements with her. These may include letters and photos once or twice a year, or possibly periodic visitation if that is an agreement with which you are comfortable. Some birthmothers don't wish to have any post-birth contact, but these or other options should be discussed and agreed to before the baby has gone home with your family.

When my clients ask me about their obligations to their birthmothers after the release of the baby to them, or after their adoptions are final, my response is always the same. Please do not make a promise you are not committed to keeping.

Most families have an idea of what might work for them before being matched. However, sometimes that can change after meeting your birthmother. You may feel very comfortable with her and like to consider more openness than planned. Or, you may decide you are not comfortable with as much contact as you thought. Whatever your decision, be sure it is clearly communicated to the birthmother and your legal representative prior to taking the baby home. It's very important to have a clear and certain agreement, so there is no doubt about expectations after you're home with your baby.

A post-adoption agreement can be drawn up by your attorney, and signed by you and the baby's birthparents. This agreement will be based on honor on your part. Therefore, it is important you are very clear about what works for your family and commit only to that. Birthmothers can go to court if you have not followed through, and the judge may strongly urge you to honor your agreement.

It is important to state here, that above all else, you must remember this is the woman who gave you her child; a human being, and a part of her. Unfortunately, we have had families who have expressed as a result of what I assume is fear, a lack of respect, and even disdain for their birthmothers. I find it difficult to work with people who are unbending in this philosophy. Many are unwilling to meet her or to provide any financial support, and have, on occasion, given me lists of reasons why a birthmother should be grateful to them for taking her baby. I have heard such comments as, "Do I have to pay for food for her other children, as well as for her?" "She got herself pregnant. Why do I have to take financial responsibility for that?" One woman even refused to pay for any anesthetic during labor. These comments are disheartening and difficult to hear.

For me, they reflect a lack of understanding of the process of adoption, and much worse, contempt for the person who will give them the most important gift they can ever receive.

My belief is this attitude concerning the birthmother will translate to your child and his/her relationship to his adoption, birth family, his roots, and to you. This can only be destructive.

In our opinion, this is the person in your life who should be highly honored. I don't think those who express these opinions are basically unkind. I believe they do not understand the tremendous sacrifice involved in placing a baby for adoption. They may be focused on the loss associated with years of infertility. It may be intensified because this woman is able to give birth when, despite years of attempting to conceive, that privilege is so easily accomplished in others. Whatever the reason, they are receiving the baby they so want, due to the courage and strength of their birthmothers. Thankfully, most people get to this in time. Although we usually try to keep our opinions silent, this is an area that arouses the need to speak out.

The good news is, in my experience, most adoptive parents do follow through with whatever agreement has been made, and are happy to do so. There are no rules on what promises you must make. You need to follow your own guidance about what works for your family. Some birthmothers want families who are not interested in contact. Some want lots of contact and most are in the middle somewhere. If you do not want contact post-birth, it is best to wait for a birthmother with the same requirements. The fits that work best are the ones where post-birth contact desires are the same and clearly defined, for birthmother and family.

Our agreements with the birthmothers of our 3 children are all different. Jimmy's birthmother had many difficulties. Before he was born, we agreed to photos and letters once or twice a year.

We felt it was best for Jimmy to have no physical contact with her because of her lifestyle and her circumstances. Throughout the years, we had phone contact periodically and we sent the promised correspondences. When Jimmy turned 18, we told him he could decide on the level of contact he wished to have with her; dependent of course, upon her agreement. At that time, he opted to talk with her on the phone once or twice. During those conversations, he decided he was not at a point where he wanted to continue contact. Jimmy is 22 now, and he has recently re-established contact with his birthmother. They talk periodically, and it seems to be working for both of them. Her life is stable now, and I think they're both glad for the opportunity to get to know each other.

When Charlie was born, we were very grateful for his birthmother's willingness to share information with us regarding his Korean roots and culture. We have enormous respect for her and her courage in placing him with us. For the first several years, she sent regular birthday and holiday cards, along with bits of Korean culture enclosed. We talked periodically;

although she was embarrassed about her inability to speak English well.

When Charlie was 7, she said she needed to take some time away from her involvement with our family and with Charlie. This was sad because Charlie, even though he had not met her, felt a strong affinity for her, and has felt the loss of contact. We hope that, when she is ready, she will re-establish a relationship with us and with him. She would be so proud if she could see who he is, and we feel the loss of our ability to share all of that with her.

Nika's family is an active part of her/our lives. We have known them since our experience with Nika's sister, our daughter Emma (highlighted in this book.) There are so many reasons we love having them involved with her. She has a large birth family; all of whom love her. Nika is African American and has an African American grandma.

We can't give her that, and we have always believed you can't have too many grandmas. All of her birth family is respectful of us as her family and it is and has been a wonderful experience having them as part of Nika's life.

Every relationship between birthparents and adoptive parents is unique and individual. There is no right or wrong method of contact. You and she will know, when the time comes to make this decision, what will work best for all involved.

It's good to have an idea in mind of what you would like, but it's important to be open if your birthmother's situation and wishes differ slightly from yours. Always do what is right for your family, but look to see if there's room for adjustment if circumstances dictate.

It's a gift for me to catch up with our families and get updates about their birthmothers. Some birthmothers have not been able to change the difficult circumstances in their lives. Many have gone on to finish school, gotten married and begun their families, or have gotten jobs and are moving on to living fulfilling and happy lives. It's a blessing to them to know their babies are happy and healthy and living the lives they wanted for them.

Of course, you, as a family, are the ones with the responsibility to decide when or if your children will have contact with, or meet their birthparents until they are adults. Some families feel comfortable with early contact; some want their children to have reached 18 before they have access to that information.

One of our early matches was between a birthmother, Dorothy, who came to us from an attorney. He had worked with her on an earlier placement. She had been addicted to drugs, and had been living in a cardboard box on the street. She was 41 years old and in jail at the time we met her. Dorothy had a 20-year-old son, from whom she was estranged.

Her disposition was contrary and defensive, and she had obviously had a difficult life. She knew she was unable to parent and wanted to place her baby with a family who would be willing to work with her.

One of our families was undaunted by her history and asked to meet her. Upon doing so, they told us they felt that under the defensive and sometimes hostile attitude, there was a frightened woman who wanted to do the right thing for her child. As they moved forward, all of us were inspired by Gwen's and Tony's continual support of her. When she was released from jail, they found a rehab program for her, and helped her furnish her small room. Gwen even made curtains. Dorothy's medical care was meticulously handled by Gwen and we gradually began to see small changes in Dorothy. She began to soften.

Shortly before their match, my close friend, Jane, who was a producer for a large national news network, called to tell me the network was interested in following an adoption plan from beginning to end. When I mentioned this to Gwen and her husband Tony, they expressed interest; and when Dorothy was asked, she agreed.

We all watched, as the match unfolded and as the cameras followed Dorothy and Gwen and Tony on their journey to the birth of their baby. We went along as they all took a trip to the beach, and the two women sat together on the sand, talking about Dorothy's life and her wish for her baby to break the cycle of her history.

We were there for the ultrasound when Gwen and Tony found out their baby was a girl, and we were all there, with the news team as Dorothy delivered her baby girl after a long labor. We saw her relief as she watched Gwen and Tony's love and care for their daughter.

A year or so later, we all gathered again, as the news crew filmed Dorothy's reunion with her family, and her 21-year-old son, whom she had not seen for many years. A couple of years later, Dorothy married, and Gwen and Tony and their daughter were there to share her day with her and her new husband.

Over the years, their contact with Dorothy has diminished. We have heard that she has slipped back into some of her old behaviors. However, we all think of her often and we all feel privileged to have been allowed to share the time we had with her and to watch her journey for a while. Gwen and Tony's daughter, Elizabeth, is now a teen, and is a beautiful, bright, happy young girl with loving parents and a younger sister adopted a year after her birth.

It is hard to understand, until you have met your birthmother, how this relationship will impact your life. It will be different from any other relationship. For us, the love we feel for the three women who allowed us to parent our children, is deep and constant. When I think of them, it is always with deep gratitude and love; and, in Jimmy's case, a fair amount of frustration.

Jimmy's birthmother presented challenges and made the time between the match, his birth, and finalization of his adoption, very difficult. She had been addicted to cocaine and was prostituting to fund her habit. She constantly threatened to keep or take him back. She refused to eat almost anything nourishing, and there were no loving gestures toward him prior to the birth. There were times we felt angry and hurt by things she said and did. In retrospect, we realize her behavior was a result of her own life circumstances that made it difficult for her to function in the world. She had a difficult childhood; with a father who was addicted to heroin and a mother who was distracted and somewhat absent. Despite knowing all that, at the time, we were feeling helpless and vulnerable to her whims.

We had waited so long for our baby; we could barely tolerate her manipulations. It wasn't easy to understand or forgive some of the problems she created.

Over the years, his birthmother, Christine, has placed 4 babies including Jimmy, for adoption because of her habit. The older 2 sisters were taken as babies before Jimmy's birth and placed with their paternal grandmother. After Jimmy's birth, and when we had some time to take a step back and look at the situation rationally, we were able to gain some perspective and compassion for her. At that point, we began to be able to have peace and joy in sending the pictures and letters that always meant so much to her.

What Do We Do If The Birthmother Calls?

Sometimes birthmothers just need to hear that all is well with the family and the baby. They need reassurance they've made the right decision and the baby is where he/she is supposed to be. This may create stress and fear, and it will probably feel threatening. Our belief is it's important to let her know all is well and how happy you are, and express your gratitude again for the priceless gift she's given you. In most cases, this is the affirmation she needs. Reaffirm whatever your agreement is regarding photos, letters or visits, and express your care and concern for her.

Under most circumstances, that will give her additional peace about her decision.

If the calls continue, outside of what you've agreed, contact your adoption professionals and ask for their guidance and assistance. Ask them to get involved and help resolve whatever is motivating the extra contact. They can then work with her to help her locate whatever support is needed.

Please note, this is rarely an issue. Don't make this or any decision that has to do with your adoption plan, around fear. Most often she is not aware of the boundaries necessary after the placement. These can usually be easily resolved.

Remember What Your Birthmother Is Giving You

The idea and process of adopting a baby automatically places you in a vulnerable position. Your urgent wish for family may mean depending on someone whose life may be unstable; who may feel angry she is in this situation, etc. Those feelings may be acted out on you. During that time, it is most important to remember you are going home with a baby. She is not. Knowing she cannot care for the child she is carrying evokes some strong emotions in some women. She is not actually angry with, or aiming it at you. Because you are getting the baby, you are just the recipient. And at that time, you need to gather your internal resources and focus on remembering what she is giving to your family. Compassion and tolerance are the key words. And, they remain the key words throughout your adoption process and after. Remember, you have your child because of this woman's courage and sacrifice. And, whatever issues arise should be shared with the adoption professionals involved so they can help resolve them.

Remember what your birthmother has given you, and let the love for the gift translate to the person. She will always be in your heart. Let that guide your actions.

11.

What Do We Tell The Baby About Being Adopted, And When?

Should The Baby Know He/She Is Adopted?

Most experts agree, it is important for a child to know she is adopted. If she is not told and discovers the truth as she grows older, it seems to the child that there is some negative reason the information was withheld. Children can turn this on themselves. They imagine it must have been kept a secret because there was something negative about being adopted. Therefore, there must be something bad about or wrong with them. If he is old enough to understand he had a birthmother who placed him with (gave him to) another family to raise, he will most probably wonder why his birthmother didn't keep him. The next thought, if he has not been told about his history and the reasons his birthmother placed him, would be to assume she didn't want him. That leads back to the thought there must be something wrong with him. Of course, none of that is accurate; but to a child's mind, that would be the logical reasoning.

When And How Do We Tell Him/Her?

It's widely believed it's best to begin telling a child about how happy you are she is yours and how much you love her, immediately, from the moment you first see/hold her. There are many wonderful books for babies and young children about adoption, and it's recommended you begin reading them to your baby as soon as you bring her home. "We're so happy we adopted you." The more a child's adoption story becomes natural to her, the more it becomes a much more minor issue emotionally.

When Jimmy was about 3, he asked his daddy, "When were you adopted, Daddy?" My husband picked him up and said, "Well, some people are born into their families, and some are adopted into their families. I was born into my family and you were adopted into ours."

Jimmy thought for a moment, then looked at Daddy and said, "Okay" then wiggled to get down and ran back to his play. Daddy's answer felt natural to him and he processed it on his level, and then moved on to what he was doing.

It's also important as a child gets older and can begin to understand, to talk with him about the fact he had a birthmother who carried him in her tummy. "Mommy couldn't carry you in her tummy, so a wonderful lady carried you in hers. She knew how much we wanted you and she let us be your mommy and daddy."

This story will be embellished with the facts, as the child grows, but age appropriate is the key. You will know your child better than anyone and you'll know when she is ready to begin to know her story; and I believe, it's best to tell it in stages. Start with simple facts at the beginning and give more details as she grows. There are wonderful resource books to help guide you about how to approach this with your child. Children's books are available, beginning at infancy and up for each age group. These books are a great way to begin the conversation and are excellent tools to assist you in the discussion about your child's history and adoption. Cuddling up and reading together is a lovely way to share communication about this deeply personal topic.

What Do We Tell Him/Her About His/Her Birthmother?

Again, most of this will be determined considering what the child is ready to hear, and what is appropriate regarding the individual conditions that contributed to his adoption and his birthmother's situation at the time.

Each birthmother is an individual and has her own life conditions, story, and reason for placing her baby. She may be a very young girl and unable to care for a child, or she may be a college student who wants to continue her schooling and get established before she becomes a parent. She may have other children and may be receiving no physical or financial support. She may, then, feel she is unable, at this time, to add another child to her family.

There are as many stories as birthmothers. Obviously, these examples don't begin to cover the spectrum of circumstances. Whatever her situation, there is a family for her baby.

I've been involved in hundreds of adoptions, and my belief is these little ones always go where they are supposed to go. One other thing I firmly believe is every birthmother who places a baby is doing so because she wants the best for her baby. Whatever her circumstances, this has got to be one of the most difficult things she will ever do. What makes her able to do it is her love for her baby and wish for the baby to have the best life possible. She is making this choice to give her baby all she is unable to provide at this time.

One of our birthmothers, during a conversation where she was describing how difficult it was going to be for her to place her baby, said to me, "I'm having such a hard time with this decision. But this morning I began to realize that where I am in my life, now, I'm not capable of giving my baby the life I want her to have. I think that sometimes being a good and responsible parent means not parenting."

When you talk with your child about his birthmother, please remember her sacrifice and courage, and tell the story with that thought uppermost in your mind. If you tell the story with love, that emotion will translate to your child.

About Best Gift Adoptions

Nikki Biers and her husband, Michael, are the Directors of Best Gift Adoptions, Inc., a California State registered adoption facilitation office. Nikki has been working in adoption for over 20 years, and since they opened the first of their two adoption offices in 1995, have had the privilege of participating in the adoptions of over 250 babies.

Their philosophy is:

Whenever we have the opportunity to be with or hold a beautiful new baby, we are reminded what a privilege it is to do our work. We are so honored to participate in watching families come together and to see the joy when parents see their new little one for the first time. Of course, they are all the most beautiful baby ever born, and they grow into the smartest, cutest, brightest, most delicious ever. We are grateful, every day to be a part of their lives and watch them grow.

We also feel fortunate to share in this miraculous process, and to work with the courageous women whose strength and love for their babies allow us all to become families.

Nikki and Michael are the parents of three adopted children, ages 22, 20 and 15, all of whom joined their family at birth.

For more information, please contact
Best Gift Adoptions
5080 Fallbrook Ave., Woodland Hills, CA 91364
(818) 888-4333, www.bestgiftadoptions.com

Made in the USA
Charleston, SC
19 August 2012